Invitation to

SAILING

BY ALAN BROWN

Illustrated by Hervey Garrett Smith

A FIRESIDE BOOK
Published by Simon & Schuster
New York London Toronto Sydney Tokyo Singapore

ISBN 0-671-21134-X
Library of Congress Catalog Card Number 62-9596
Manufactured in the United States of America

40 39 38 37 36 35 34 33 32

Dedicated to
Junior Sailors everywhere, especially
Laurie, Jennifer, Douglas and Carolyn
— and my first mate, Nancy

CONTENTS

THE LORE OF SAILING

There is witchery in the sea, its songs and stories, and in
the mere sight of a ship, and the sailor's dress . . . the very
creaking of a block . . . and many are the boys, in every
seaport, who are drawn away, as by an almost irresistible
attraction, from their work and schools, and hang about
the decks and yards of vessels, with a fondness which, it
is plain, will have its way.

— RICHARD HENRY DANA, JR.
Two Years Before the Mast, 1840

THE *"witchery in the sea"* is a magic which has worked on mankind
since the dawn of civilization. Throughout history men have answered
its call, whether in the stately full-rigged ships of yesteryear or the
smallest catboat on the inland lakes of today. From your first look at a
sail, your first venture on the water, and that first feel of wind on your
cheek, you are a part of it. From then on your every moment revolves
around the time you can spend with your boat.

The thrill of sailing and putting out in a boat cannot be expressed
in words. It is the feeling of power and the awe of making the wind
do your work . . . or putting your strength to the severest test of man
and rigging. It is the aesthetic appeal of a beautiful hull and a bleached
sail. And it is the quiet noise of water sloshing against the prow as you
rest in your berth in the forecastle, absorbing a lifetime of memories.

But sailing is more than this.

It is mastery of a skill. It is technique. It is competition, with wind
or man or both. It is racing and striving and relaxing. It is the puff of
smoke from the cannon and the muffled sound which follows to tell
you that you've won the race. It is the dry mouth, squinting eyes, the
sunburned brow and nose. It is faces seen and friendships renewed,
year after year in regatta after regatta.

Yet the basic mystery is there. The love of the sea and its lore.
Ingrained. Never lost. Dormant but not dead, it returns to the old man
showing his grandsons a back splice, a knot, a carved figurehead . . .
or spinning a yarn of schooners and luggers and crashing spume and
tossing seas.

INTRODUCTION

THE PURPOSE of this book is to make simple the fundamentals of sailing. Few people are privileged to have the help of a sailing instructor when they are starting out. This book can be your instructor.

The techniques and principles of sailing are presented in lesson form . . . lessons derived from years of instructing pupils and classes, of using trial and error methods, and of finding out what works easiest, safest and best. These will give you the basic groundwork you need to sail safely and with confidence.

The lessons progress according to skills. For the sailor who has some knowledge of fundamentals, racing is brought in as soon as possible. It is here you find some of the greatest pleasures in the sport. Besides, there is no great mystery to racing boats, and in these pages you will find the steps to racing simple and clear.

The intricate details have been left out. You can find them in many other books on sailing. Here are the fundamentals you need to know for a lifetime of pleasure in the world's finest sport.

Good luck, and have many fine cruises!

HOW TO USE THIS BOOK

1. Follow each lesson in order. Start at the beginning of the book and work through each lesson progressively. This will assure you of the basic skills needed to master the more advanced sections. Even if you have a general knowledge of boats, it won't hurt to review fundamentals. Who knows, you may find something you really didn't understand before!

2. Do the written exercises at the end of each chapter. These help test what you have learned. If you have questions, or can't give an answer, look it up. All of the exercises cover basic material that you should know.

3. Follow the on-the-water drills. These drills let you put your theory to work. Sail with a friend or someone in your family; if possible, with someone who has had some experience and can show you the ropes.

4. Follow all safety measures. Don't go out when there are whitecaps on the water. Don't go out without a life jacket for each person in the boat. Don't go out if you can't swim.

5. Learn the basic knots. In Part I, each chapter has a small section devoted to a knot, splice, or bit of seamanship. Learn a new one with each lesson.

6. Use the book in groups. If you are fortunate enough to be in a sailing class, you will find the book ideal for classes. Lessons can be covered in one or two class sessions. Do your reading at home and bring your questions to your instructor. He will decide your on-the-water drills according to the weather.

7. How the book is divided. The book consists of three parts. In Part I you will find the basic fundamentals of sailing and an introduction to racing. A mastery of these precepts — as shown by the check list at the end of the section — will mean you are a qualified sailing skipper and able to handle a boat on your own with confidence.

Part II is for the intermediate sailor, and deals with the Marconi-rigged boat (two sails), and with racing strategy, basic tactics, regattas, and boat maintenance.

Part III is a unique section for the sponsoring group, yacht club, and sailing instructor. It concerns the organization of sailing fleets and classes, and discusses methods of teaching sailing.

PART I

HOW TO SAIL

Start sailing — start racing! You can become a competent sailor only with a good working knowledge of the reasons why a boat moves under sail and of the limitations that it has.

To acquire this knowledge, you first have to "speak the language" and know the names of the boat's parts and the names of boating maneuvers. You have to develop certain reflexes, so that steering a course or trimming a sail becomes instinctive.

You must develop a sixth sense for weather signs. You must know about wind . . . and how to use it for safe sailing. Last comes the thrill of racing. Here, basic seamanship counts the most, and here you can practice it with most advantage and fun. There are a few simple "rules of the road" to learn, and the rest is easy.

Where do you start? Why, with a boat of course!

1. Basic Seamanship

1. Choosing your boat. You will get the most satisfaction from the boat you choose to own if it suits your needs and the kind of sailing you want to do.

If you just plan to putter about in a sailboat now and then, almost any simply designed boat will be all right. If you feel you may want to do some racing later on, you will want the type of boat that other people in your area have so there will be people to race against.

If you don't live near water and will have to tow your boat on a trailer or the car roof, get one that is small enough to carry and handle easily. On the other hand, if you plan to keep your boat moored in the water, be sure it is big enough and sturdy enough to withstand any storms in your area.

What size boat? The most important consideration here is how much you know about sailing and how much experience you have had on the water. If you have not sailed before except as a passenger on someone's boat now and then, you will want to start with a small boat that is easy to sail and easy to care for. The larger boats look nice — and you can dream all you want to about taking your friends out with you, having parties, etc. — but you will find they are harder to sail and more work to care for. All boats need cleaning, painting, hauling out, tying up, care through the winter, and more. Few fair-weather friends help here . . . it will be mostly up to you.

In addition, the smaller boats respond more easily to changes in the wind, are easier to steer, and harder to get into trouble or do any real damage to. A skipper who learns in them will know more about sailing and wind and seamanship by far than those who try to start too big. Many an enthusiastic boatman has been deceived and disappointed by buying a large, expensive boat, only to find he cannot sail it safely and it is too large to be cared for easily.

How small is a small boat? The best size for young beginners is the 8- to 12-foot length. There are literally hundreds of different designs of boats this size. Usually they have one sail — these are the best. When many boats are made with the same design, all to look alike, they are called *class boats*. The class is then given a name and its insignia is put on the sails, like a Penguin, Moth, Sabot, or Pram.

If you are an adult or large person, get a boat that is big enough to be comfortable. Although two adults can manage in an 8-foot dinghy, they will be more comfortable in one 10 or 12 feet long.

Dinghies are any small boats without decks and with one sail or two. They include most of the class boats in the 8- to 10-foot lengths. The word *dinghy* is also used in referring to a small rowboat, or tender.

How much money for a new boat? Most small boats are economical. Dinghies may be bought in kit form for as low as $45, with the pieces all cut out to size, and including everything except sails, mast, and boom. Complete kits for 10- to 12-foot boats will run about $125 to $300, plus an additional $35 to $95 for nylon sails, depending on size. A few tools and a week's work will put you on the water. The more expensive kits have their parts in a more finished condition, so your work is simpler.

Prices for new boats in these lengths run from $300 to $500 without sails.

The secondhand boat. If you are just getting started in sailing, your best buy for the money is a secondhand boat. Boats do not lose value and depreciate as do automobiles. A ten- or fifteen-year-old boat which has had reasonably good care is nearly as satisfactory as a new one. Also, the secondhand boat has taken a few knocks, and you won't feel so badly if you give it a few more.

Look around the area where you will be sailing. If there are class boats there, a secondhand one will be inexpensive and you will be able to resell it more easily than if you bring in an unknown type of boat.

Plastic or wooden hull? This is a question you will ask yourself if you are considering a boat. Most dinghies today are built of either marine plywood or fiberglass. Plywood is made in thin layers bound with waterproof glue, and is exceptionally strong and durable. Like all wood, it needs painting and may crack or chip, or even rot. But with ordinary care it will do very well.

Wooden boats 12 to 18 feet long are often made of wooden boards in strips or planks, rather than plywood. If the wood is seasoned and lightweight, and the boat made by a good builder, these planked hulls are excellent. Cedar is often used because of its strength and light weight.

In the past ten years, the development of plastic hulls has changed the entire boat-building industry. The most successful are the fiberglass hulls. Fiberglass is a spun-glass material which is processed into a tough, lightweight, rot-proof hull with the color built in. It won't need painting and needs very little care. The main disadvantage is in repairing fittings, or putting new fittings in, where the rock-hard fiberglass is difficult to drill or work with. If a break or crack develops, it takes a special process to fix it . . . but it happens so seldom you will probably not need a repair kit.

For the money spent, a fiberglass hull is a good buy in a boat 8 to 14 feet long.

2. What to look for in a secondhand boat. A good general rule to follow in checking a used boat is to examine all the places where the boat takes a strain.

On the hull. This would be where the various wire fittings (stays and shrouds) fasten to the deck, where the mast is held and where the bottom of it rests. Look for loose screws and cracks in the wood. At the front of the hull, check for cracks or filled areas or other signs of collision. In the rear, look at the metal fittings which hold the rudder. Have the owner put the rudder on, and see that it turns easily without a lot of loose "play."

Inside the hull. Look at the very bottom, especially around the centerboard trunk (the large boxlike structure in the middle). Shake the trunk and see if it is at all loose. It should not be. Test the wood in the bottom with your fingernail or the small blade of a penknife. If the wood is soft and "punky," chances are good that it has *dry rot.* This is a fungus infection which invades wood, turning it to a dry and chalky material inside while keeping the outer painted edges intact. Don't worry about the deck and a few chips or gouges here and there. They can be readily fixed.

The mast and boom should be examined for cracks and for evidence of splitting or rotting at the points where the rigging is fastened on. Sight along the mast to see that it is straight and not warped. Again, test the wood in any suspicious areas, using a small blade. Don't worry about varnish, you can redo it. If the mast is badly stained (from lack of varnish), chances are the boat has had poor care, and you should be extra careful in your inspection.

Look at all the extra gear. This includes rudder, tiller, and centerboard especially. Look over all the ropes and ask where they are used. Run them through your hands from one end to the other and check for worn spots, broken strands, and frayed areas. Worn ropes will have to be replaced. You will need a paddle, life jackets (not cushions), small anchor, anchor line, bailing can, and sponge . . . so see if these are included and what condition they are in.

Sails should be opened up and laid out on the floor. The parts that get the strain here are the corners and the two edges which have a rope (bolt rope) sewn into the hem. This rope should not be worn through at any place. Tears at the corners, especially around the eyelets which are built in, will have to be repaired.

The color of the sail will give you an idea of its age, as the older sail tends to become white and gray. The new cotton sail is almost yellow-white in color. Synthetic sails, like Orlon, nylon, and Dacron will not change. Stained areas on cotton sails are probably mildew, a sign of age and poor strength. It too is a fungus infection, caused by leaving sails damp when storing them. Synthetic sails will not mildew. Patches, if good ones, will make little difference.

An older sail (in the five- to eight-year or older group) is a poor buy. By this time a sail has lost much of its shape and is only good for hard winds and stormy weather. For small boats synthetic sails are the best investment for the beginner.

3. The basic sailboat. The simplest boat is rigged with one mast, a boom, and one sail. This is called a *catboat*. It is the best type of boat to start sailing in.

By "rig" is meant the number of masts, booms, sails and supporting wires on a boat. Figure 1 shows some different types of catboat rigs. Most catboats have a small deck, but if not, we call them *dinghies*.

Your boat may have a second, smaller sail up front. This is a

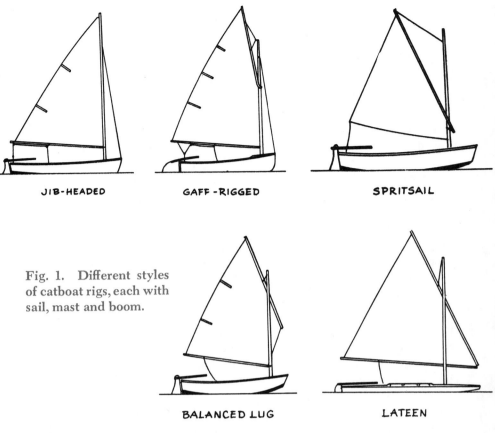

JIB-HEADED   GAFF-RIGGED   SPRITSAIL

Fig. 1. Different styles of catboat rigs, each with sail, mast and boom.

BALANCED LUG   LATEEN

jib (rhymes with rib), and changes the rig to a *sloop*. If you are just learning to sail, take your jib off and leave it ashore. Most small boats will sail just as well without it, and you will learn your fundamentals much more easily and quickly without having to bother with two sails. The sloop rig will be discussed in Chapter 10.

The hull. This is the main body of your boat, and certain parts of it you should know by name. (See Fig. 2.)

When in the boat, you will be sitting either on the *floorboards,* the *thwart* (seat), or up on the *gunwale* (gun'l), the upper edge of the hull.

The spars. These are the *mast* and *boom.* They are joined together by a metal fitting called a *gooseneck,* which allows the boom to swing up and down and sideways (Fig. 5). The sail attaches to the mast by a slot, or by slides on a track. Your boat will have one or the other.

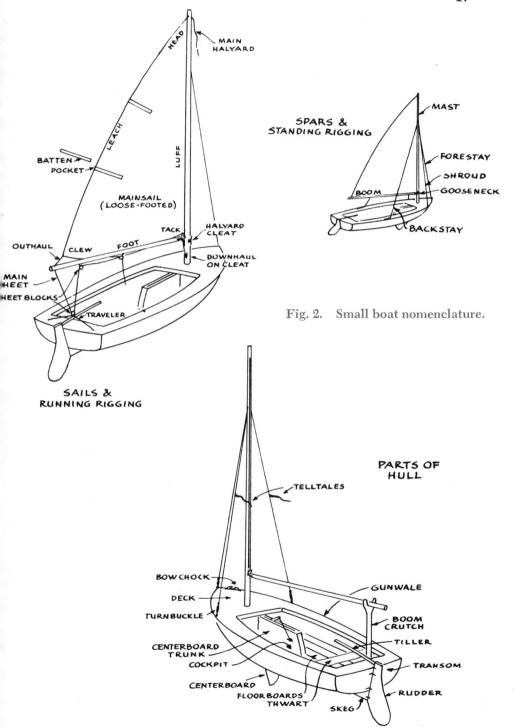

HEAD

MAIN HALYARD

LEACH

BATTEN POCKET

LUFF

MAINSAIL (LOOSE-FOOTED)

OUTHAUL

CLEW

FOOT

TACK

HALYARD CLEAT

DOWNHAUL ON CLEAT

MAIN SHEET

SHEET BLOCKS

TRAVELER

SAILS & RUNNING RIGGING

SPARS & STANDING RIGGING

MAST

FORESTAY

SHROUD

GOOSENECK

BOOM

BACKSTAY

Fig. 2.   Small boat nomenclature.

PARTS OF HULL

TELLTALES

BOW CHOCK

DECK

TURNBUCKLE

CENTERBOARD TRUNK

COCKPIT

CENTERBOARD

FLOORBOARDS THWART

SKEG

GUNWALE

BOOM CRUTCH

TILLER

TRANSOM

RUDDER

The standing rigging. Almost all boats have some wire guys or supports for the mast. These are called the *standing rigging*, because they are fixed in position and don't move. The wires that support the mast sideways are called *shrouds*. Those that support it the length of the boat are called *stays*. The stays are named for the part of the boat they attach to; for example, there is a headstay, jibstay, and backstay, depending on how large the boat is (Fig. 2).

The running rigging. All the manila or wire ropes that *move* on the boat, to haul the sail up and down, etc., are called *running rigging*. These include the *halyards* (hal-yerds), which hoist the sails, and the *sheets*, which are fastened to the boom and pull the sail in and out (Fig. 2).

Your sheet is fastened to the boom by means of small pulleys, called *blocks*. One of these blocks may slide on a rod or wire which goes across the back of your boat. This is a sheet *traveler* (Fig. 2).

The helm. This is a term you will hear often around boats. It means the steering mechanism or the thing you steer with on a boat. On dinghies the helm consists of a rudder and tiller (Fig. 2). The *tiller* is always the part you hold onto, and the *rudder* is the section in the water. On larger yachts the helm may consist of a ship's wheel attached to the rudder by steering cables.

The centerboard. All boats need a centerboard or *keel* (Fig. 3) to keep them sailing straight and to keep them from tipping over (see Chapter 2). Dinghies usually have a centerboard, which is a flat plate of metal or wood which goes through the boxlike structure in the middle of your boat (the *centerboard trunk*) and extends below the surface.

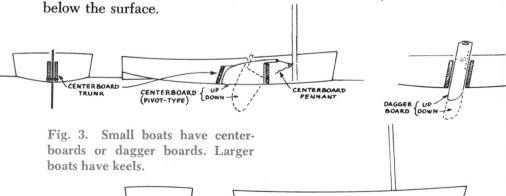

Fig. 3. Small boats have centerboards or dagger boards. Larger boats have keels.

Centerboards are of two types. The *pivoting* board is hinged by a small pin at the front of the trunk, and when pulled up also swings to the rear. *Dagger* boards go straight down, take up less room than pivoting boards, and are equally satisfactory.

4. Parts of the sail. The sail is named by its corners and edges. These names are easy to remember, and you will need to know them in order to read about the fundamentals of sailing.

Edges. The forward or leading edge is the *luff* (Fig. 2). When this part of the sail shakes, it is known as *luffing*. The bottom edge is the *foot* and the trailing edge (the wide curved part) is the *leach*. Some people mistakenly call this the roach. The *roach* is merely the degree of curve to the leach.   *Leech*

Corners. The top corner is the *head,* and it has a wooden piece sewn in to strengthen it, called a *headboard.* This is where the halyard attaches. The bottom forward corner is the *tack* and the rear corner is the *clew.*

Outhaul and downhaul. These are lines which adjust the foot of the sail, down along the mast and out along the boom.

The *outhaul* pulls the sail tight along the boom, and fastens to a cleat on the boom (Fig. 4). The *downhaul* (Fig. 5) moves the boom and gooseneck down, and attaches to a cleat (metal or wooden fastener) on the side of the mast.

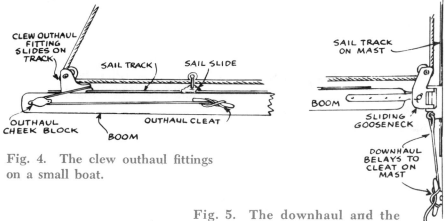

Fig. 4.   The clew outhaul fittings on a small boat.

Fig. 5.   The downhaul and the gooseneck.

Loose-footed sail. Some catboats have a groove, or a slide and track along the boom to hold foot of sail. Many do not, and will attach the sail only by the tack at the gooseneck and by the clew outhaul at the end of the boom. This is a *loose-footed* sail.

Battens. These are small pieces of wood, inserted into pockets on the leach or foot of the sail, to keep it flatter at these points. Some sails have battens sewn in permanently, some slide out to make sail easier to stuff into the sail bag.

Bolt rope, cringle, and shackles. To take some of the strain off the sail, a tarred rope is sewn into the hem along the foot and luff. This is the *bolt rope.* At the corners where lines or halyards fasten, there is a ring or hole lined with rope or metal. This is a *cringle.* Through the cringle you may put a *shackle,* a U-shaped piece of metal with a pin, which fastens your halyard to the sail, or the tack of the sail to the gooseneck. Tie a small piece of cord to your shackle pins to keep them from falling overboard.

5. Readying the boat for sailing. This will mean putting on the sail, fastening the rudder and tiller, lowering the centerboard, etc.

The fittings which attach these parts are slightly different on every boat, depending on size and class, and each sailor learns how the parts on his boat work. What is important in getting ready to sail is the *order* in which you do things.

Let's see what the order would be for a typical small dinghy, assuming you have already *stepped the mast* (put it on and fastened rigging) and attached the boom.

(1) *Place all gear in boat.* This will be life jackets for you and your crew, sail bag with sail, paddle, rudder, tiller, bailing can or scoop, sponge, and your *ditty bag* (small bag of personal items: sunglasses, sun lotion, Band-aids, knife, pliers, screw driver, string, piece of wire, etc.).

(2) *Launch boat.* Carry your boat to the launching ramp or beach and *lower* it into the water. Do not scrape on shore. Take the line from the front of the boat and tie it up at the pier. Make sure front of boat points *into* the wind.

(3) *Lower centerboard.* When the boat is tied up, step into the

cockpit and lower the centerboard at once. This gives boat stability, and prevents tipping over at the dock. CAUTION: Always get into a small boat by stepping directly into the bottom of the cockpit, not on the seat or the gunwale. Otherwise you may tip it over.

(4) *Fasten rudder and tiller.* Put on the rudder and swing it vigorously to make sure it is secure. The tiller should be put under the traveler or main sheet before it is fastened with the tiller pin.

(5) *Put on the sail.* Sailors call this "bending on the sail," as the word "bend" means to tie on.

(a) *First, find the headboard* of your sail. Then take your halyard, look aloft and see that it is clear and not wrapped around mast or rigging, and shackle it to the head of the sail.

(b) *Overhaul the sail* by running your hands along the bolt rope, beginning at the head where you have attached the halyard. Take out any twists.

(c) *Insert slides* on the mast as you are overhauling sail, starting with top slide. When they are all on, tie a piece of cord around mast to keep them from sliding down.

(d) *Fasten sail at gooseneck.* Overhaul the sail along the foot, taking out twists until you come to the clew. Run the sail out the boom (put slides on, or run in slot) and attach the clew outhaul. Pull this only moderately tight, and cleat it.

(6) *Put in battens.* They should be 1 or 2 inches shorter than the pockets. Tie with a square knot. (See Fig. 38 for knot.)

(7) *Clear mainsheet.* See that the sheet runs through the proper blocks (pulleys) and is not caught on tiller or centerboard well. Find the end of the sheet and tie a figure-8 knot in the end (see Fig. 39), to keep the end from pulling through the blocks. Raise the boom above head — this will give sheet plenty of slack — and replace the boom in the boom crutch. See that the *downhaul is untied.*

(8) *Look aloft and hoist sail.* Always look up and watch the sail as you pull it up. See that the slides are not twisted and that the battens do not catch on shrouds or stays. If the sail is hard to pull up, stop pulling. See if anything is jammed, and fix it. If it looks clear, pull sail down a few inches by bolt rope, and hoist again.

As the sail nears the top, *lift the boom out of the crutch* to take weight off the sail and allow the boom to be pulled up. Hold the halyard and put the boom crutch in the cockpit so the boom can swing free in the wind.

Set up on halyard. This means pulling the sail up the last inch or two, which is usually hard to do. By holding the halyard at the cleat and pulling outward, you increase the force of your pull and will get the sail up to the top (Fig. 6).

Fig. 6.   Here is the proper way to set up on a halyard, to get sail hoisted the last difficult inch or two.

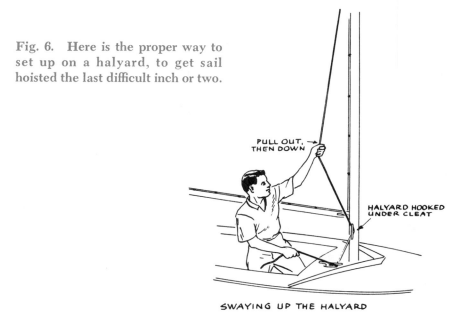

PULL OUT, → THEN DOWN

HALYARD HOOKED UNDER CLEAT

SWAYING UP THE HALYARD

Secure halyard to cleat by taking a full round turn and two or three figure-8 crosses, then finishing with one or two round turns.

Make up the halyard. A line is "made up" by coiling it so that it is ready to use again. Always lay the coils in a clockwise direction, "with the sun." Start coiling the halyard *at the cleat,* so you can shake any snarls out of the free end. Stow the coil in the bottom of boat, but turn it so the top loop will come off first when the halyard is lowered (Fig. 7).

(9) *Adjust the downhaul.* The downhaul is tightened so the luff of the sail begins to wrinkle. (Further adjustments of downhaul and outhaul will be discussed in the coming chapters.)

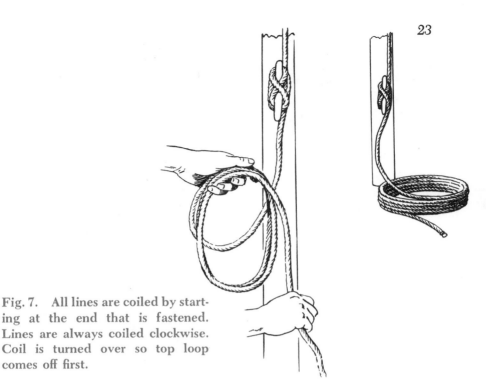

Fig. 7. All lines are coiled by starting at the end that is fastened.
Lines are always coiled clockwise.
Coil is turned over so top loop
comes off first.

If your sail fastens to the mast by running the bolt rope in a
slot, you will follow all the steps above in order, but will not attach
the sail to the mast until ready to hoist it. Be sure you have over-
hauled it along the bolt rope to take out any twists. Then have crew
carefully feed it into the slot on the mast while you hoist and look
aloft.

SUMMARY OF STEPS

IN GETTING CATBOAT READY TO SAIL:

(1) Place all gear in boat.
(2) Launch boat. Head into wind.
(3) Lower centerboard when you first get in.
(4) Fasten rudder and tiller.
(5) Put on sail: attach halyard, slides on mast, goose-
        neck, slides on boom, outhaul.
(6) Insert battens.
(7) Clear sheet. Figure-8 knot in end.
(8) Look aloft and hoist sail.
(9) Secure halyard. Secure downhaul.

6. Names of directions. There are certain names which seamen use to refer to general parts of the boat and to positions around the boat.

All positions on the boat and off it are given in relation to the way the boat is pointing (Fig. 8).

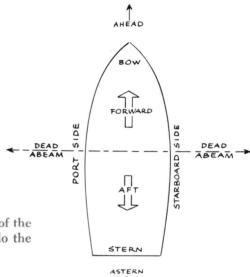

Fig. 8.   Each general section of the boat has a special name, as do the areas in the water nearby.

Starboard is the name of the right side of the boat as you face forward. Objects on the right are said to be *to starboard*.

Port is the left side, and objects on your left are said to be *to port*.

Bow (rhymes with how) is the front end, and the *stern* is the rear section. Everything in the front half is *forward*, while things in the rear are *aft*. You can move forward to the bow, or move aft to the stern.

Areas around the boat are named as shown in Figure 8. The *beam* is the widest part of the boat, but objects *abeam* are off to the side. If *dead abeam* they are at right angles to the boat.

7. Basic launching and landing. There is nothing to launching or landing a boat if you remember one simple rule: *always head into the wind whenever raising or lowering sail* (Fig. 9). This means that the wind will come onto the boat from ahead of it.

The importance of this cannot be emphasized too strongly. When the wind is blowing over your side (from abeam) or over

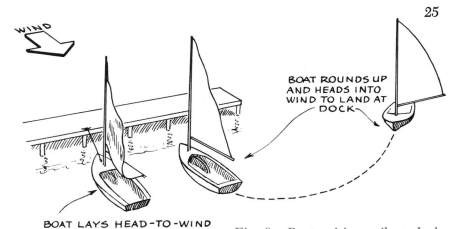

BOAT LAYS HEAD-TO-WIND
TO HOIST SAIL

Fig. 9. Boat raising sail at dock and boat landing *both* head into the wind.

your stern (from the rear), you *cannot* hoist or lower sail safely. The wind will fill the sail and prevent you from moving it up or down and will blow you against the pier, or aground.

By heading into the wind you let the sail blow out behind the mast like a weather vane. When you lower sail it drops into the boat, not the water. When you hoist it, the sail is above you blowing loosely (luffing), and not pushing you around before you are ready.

How to launch a dinghy. Launching simply means the putting of a boat into the water. Most dinghies and small boats are kept out of the water except when they are to be actually sailed. This is "dry sailing." You can rig your boat ashore, but do not hoist sail. Fold the sail on top of the boom and secure it with a turn or two of small line.

Two people can easily carry the boat to the water, or you can launch from a trailer. Don't let the bottom scratch on the sand or gravel. Use a wooden or inflated rubber roller if the boat is too heavy to carry, or slide it down a wooden launching ramp.

When in the water, paddle to a dock and prepare to hoist sail. If the wind is light, you can paddle to deep water, put on the rudder and tiller, lower the centerboard, head into the wind and raise the sail.

8. Mooring out. If you keep your boat in the water, the best place to tie it up is at a mooring. Here it can swing with the wind and tide, and not hit other boats.

Moorings are made by using a heavy anchor and some kind of float to keep the mooring line at the surface. For boats up to 25 feet, a mushroom-type anchor of 125 to 175 pounds is needed (see later chapters).

Fastening mooring line to boat. Most small boats that are moored out will have a *cleat* or a *bitt* on the deck to fasten the line to. If your boat has a cleat, then the line should also be tied around the mast. A small piece of canvas should be sewed on the anchor line at the place where it runs through your *bow chock,* to reduce wear from chafing or rubbing together.

Leaving boat for the night. Tie the halyards so both ends are fastened. Pull the sheet up tight, coil it, and hang it where it will stay dry. Raise the centerboard. Take off the rudder and tiller, or else tie the tiller in the mid-line with a piece of cord so it won't swing about. Put on a boat cover if you have one.

Picking up mooring. When you sail in to pick up your float, the same principles apply as in landing at a pier: be sure you are headed into the wind, and come in slowly so you don't sail right past it.

9. Use of the dinghy. The little tender or rowboat you may use to row out to your mooring is often called a dinghy, too. There are a few simple things to remember in using it.

Get into the dinghy by holding onto both gunwales and stepping directly into the bottom, *not* on the seat. Stepping on the gunwale will tip you over, and stepping on the seat will get it wet and dirty where you will sit. Place a sail bag on the seat to keep it dry.

Rowing the dinghy. Row with a strong but easy stroke. Do not dip oars deeply into water, but keep them just beneath the surface. On the return stroke, drop your wrists so the oars turn with the blades into the wind. This is known as "feathering the oars." It makes rowing easier, especially in a strong wind.

Approaching the moored boat. As you row alongside the boat, put your oars in the boat, and take out the *rowlock* (oarlock) on the side nearest the boat so it won't mark the side. Place the sail bag on a seat in the cockpit, tie the dinghy astern, and climb aboard. If there is water in the boat, bail it out. The cockpit cover and sail bag can be left in the dinghy tied at the mooring while you are out sailing.

10. How to take care of sails. Sail care begins as soon as you use your sail. It is important because the sail is the motor for your boat, and sails are an expensive part of the boat, as well.

Wet lines. If the halyard, downhaul, or outhaul get wet, they will shrink. This puts an added strain on the sail, and may even tear it. Whenever any lines get wet, loosen them.

Pulling sail down. If you are headed into the wind properly when you lower the sail, it will fall on the boat. Don't let the sail go overboard, as it will then have to be dried before you can put it away.

If the sail sticks on the way down, grasp it by the bolt rope and pull down gently. Later you will want to grease the slide with Vaseline or other waterproof grease to help the sail come down more easily.

Stowing the sail. Sails should be kept in sail bags and hung in a locker or closet or other dry place.

The sail may simply be stuffed into the bag, beginning with the *foot* and ending with the *head* on top, since this part will be used first when you take the sail out.

The sail can be folded, and will take up less room in the sail bag this way. Stretch it out on a dry lawn or clean pier. Begin by pulling it over in folds about 1 foot wide, like an accordion, working toward the luff (Fig. 10). Then roll from the foot, so that the head of the sail is on the outside, ready for use.

Taking care of wet sails. Sails should not be put into the sail bag when damp or wet, as the moisture hastens mildew and rot. Cotton sails should be stretched out on a lawn to dry, or, if the weather is rainy, draped loosely over chairs or a bed. Nylon, Dacron and other synthetic sails are mildew-resistant, but should be dried so that bolt ropes, outhauls, etc., do not stay wet and rot. Do not hang wet sails up by the corners. This will only stretch them out of proper shape. However, small sails can be draped across a clothes-line without harming them.

Fig. 10.   Sail is folded in layers like an accordion, then rolled from foot to head.

HEAD

AFTER FOLDING,
ROLL SAIL
TOWARD HEAD

CLEW

TACK

BASIC KNOTS AND SEAMANSHIP

Cleating a line. (Fig. 11)

Use: For fastening halyards, outhauls, downhauls. It is *never* used for fastening the sheet, as the sheet often has to be released in a hurry.

Other uses: It can be used on a cleat that fastens a mooring line, by making one or two of the figure-8 turns a locking half hitch, so the line is more securely held.

Step 1: Take full round turn around cleat.

Step 2: Cross over top of cleat to form one or two figure 8's.

Step 3: Finish with one or two full round turns, each pulled in tight.

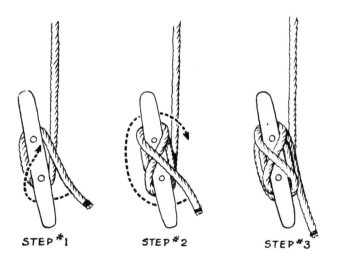

STEP *1   STEP *2   STEP *3

Fig. 11.   Cleating a line.

The jam cleat. (Fig. 12)

Use: For temporarily securing centerboard pennants, jib sheet, spinnaker guy, etc. This type of cleat will not take as much strain as the other, but can be released quickly.

Step 1: Take half a round turn on wide side.

Step 2: Pull line tight into jamming side. Pull out to release.

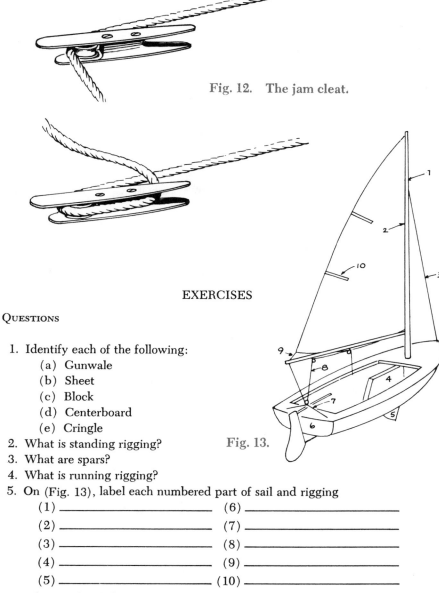

Fig. 12.   The jam cleat.

EXERCISES

1. Identify each of the following:
    (a) Gunwale
    (b) Sheet
    (c) Block
    (d) Centerboard
    (e) Cringle
2. What is standing rigging?
3. What are spars?
4. What is running rigging?
5. On (Fig. 13), label each numbered part of sail and rigging

Fig. 13.

    (1) _____   (6) _____
    (2) _____   (7) _____
    (3) _____   (8) _____
    (4) _____   (9) _____
    (5) _____   (10) _____

6. What is a boat's helm?
    What might it consist of?
7. How is the bolt rope fastened to a sail?
    Is it attached for the full length of all edges?
    Which edges of sail does it attach to?

8. Your boat is tied at the pier, and you are about to get ready to go sailing. Choose the right steps from column *B*, put them in proper order and write them in column *A*.

A	B
(1) _____	Put on sail
(2) _____	Fasten rudder and tiller
(3) _____	Clear mainsheet
(4) _____	Lower centerboard
(5) _____	Tie figure-8 knot
(6) _____	Put in battens
(7) _____	Shackle halyard
(8) _____	Look aloft, hoist sail

9. On the figure below, fill in the names of directions or positions that are missing. (Fig. 14).

(1) _____

(2) _____

(3) _____

(4) _____

(5) _____

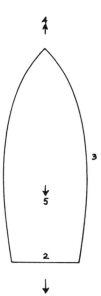

Fig. 14.

10. Answer true or false:
    (a) _____ Luffing is a shaking of the sail along the luff.
    (b) _____ Fiberglass hulls are smooth, but tend to rot.
    (c) _____ It makes no difference if sails are put away wet.
    (d) _____ Small boats with one sail are better to learn sailing in than larger, heavier boats.
    (e) _____ Stained wood showing through varnish probably means the spar or boat was not well cared for.
    (f) _____ If cotton sails become wet while sailing, outhaul and downhaul should be tightened.
    (g) _____ Sail may be pulled down gently, but only by bolt rope.
    (h) _____ Having wind abeam will make sail hoisting easier.
    (i) _____ Figure-8 knot should be put in end of halyard.
    (j) _____ The gooseneck connects tiller to boom.

PRACTICE DRILL

1. Before you buy a boat, answer this check list of questions and compare your answers to those in the chapter.
    (a) What kind of sailing will you do? Pleasure only_____ Racing _____ Every day_____ Weekends, etc. _____
    (b) Are there facilities for launching, storing, and hauling of your boat?___
    (c) Have you talked to other boat owners in your area?_____
    (d) Are you familiar with the waters you will sail in? _____
2. Inspect a sailboat on shore. Name all parts of sail and rigging. Practice putting rudder and tiller together.
3. Rig sailboat on shore, including hoisting of sail — if wind is light, and boat is heading *into* wind.
4. Take the sail off and practice folding it. Now put it back on the boat, and notice how the proper folding makes it easier to bend the sail on.
5. Practice the basic knot for this chapter, and look ahead to other knots and practice them as you can.

2. *What Makes a Sailboat Go*

To be able to sail, you have to understand why a sailboat can move in the wind, and why it can sail only in certain directions and not in others.

These directions are always dependent on the position of the wind, which is the moving force or power for your boat. Boats can sail away from the wind, across the wind, and up to a 45-degree angle into the wind, but not directly into it. Let us see why.

1. How a boat sails with the wind. It is easy to see how a boat can be blown along before the wind, like a leaf upon the water. This is called *running*. The sail is out to one side at right angles to the wind, and the boat is said to be *on a run* (Fig. 15).

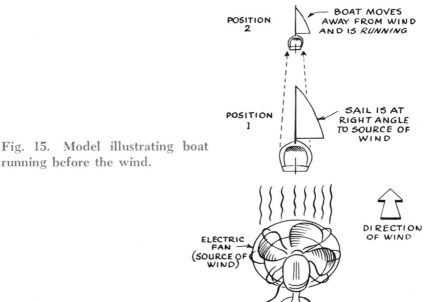

Fig. 15. Model illustrating boat running before the wind.

If the boat has a centerboard, it makes little difference if it is up or down when on a run. However, it does make a difference if the boat sails in any other direction with respect to the wind. Here is why.

2. How a boat sails across the wind. When a boat sails so that it is sideways to the wind, it is called *reaching*, and the boat is *on a reach*. Here the sail is out roughly halfway (about 45 degrees), and the centerboard must be down. The centerboard, or keel, is necessary (Fig. 16) so that the boat is not simply blown sideways down the wind, but has some resistance in the water to this sideways push (Fig. 17).

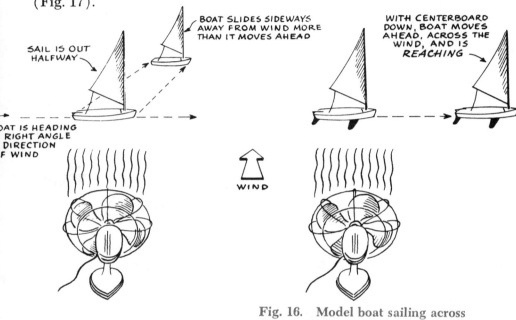

Fig. 16.   Model boat sailing across the wind on a *reach* shows need for centerboard.

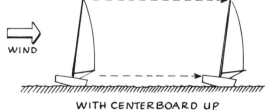

WITH CENTERBOARD UP
BOAT IS EASILY PUSHED ACROSS
SURFACE OF WATER

Fig. 17.   The centerboard or keel resists sideways push.

CENTERBOARD RESISTS
SIDEWAYS PUSH
THROUGH WATER

Lateral resistance. All parts of the boat beneath the water resist being pushed through it. When the resistance is against a sideways motion, it is called lateral resistance. This is determined by the amount of hull, keel, and centerboard which is below the water line (Fig. 18). The central point of this total area beneath the water is called the *center of lateral resistance* (Fig. 19). In general, it is thought of as a line with as much lateral area ahead of it as behind it. Knowing where this line is will help you later on when we learn how to trim a boat for faster sailing (Chapters 8 and 11).

Fig. 18.   Lateral resistance.

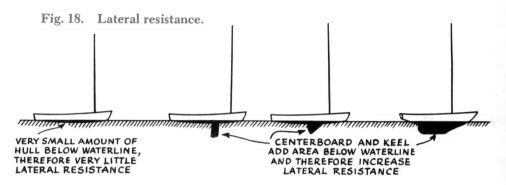

VERY SMALL AMOUNT OF
HULL BELOW WATERLINE,
THEREFORE VERY LITTLE
LATERAL RESISTANCE

CENTERBOARD AND KEEL
ADD AREA BELOW WATERLINE
AND THEREFORE INCREASE
LATERAL RESISTANCE

Forward resistance. Water resists anything moving through it, as every swimmer or diver knows. But since boats are built long and narrow, and since keels and centerboards are long and narrow, they offer much less resistance to the water (Fig. 19) moving forward than they do sideways.

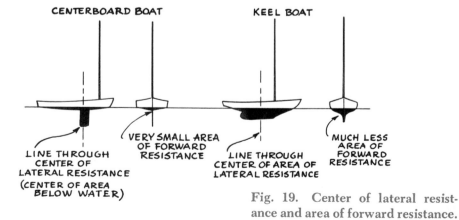

CENTERBOARD BOAT

KEEL BOAT

LINE THROUGH
CENTER OF
LATERAL RESISTANCE
(CENTER OF AREA
BELOW WATER)

VERY SMALL AREA
OF FORWARD
RESISTANCE

LINE THROUGH
CENTER OF AREA OF
LATERAL RESISTANCE

MUCH LESS
AREA OF
FORWARD
RESISTANCE

Fig. 19.   Center of lateral resistance and area of forward resistance.

Effect of the wind. Now, with the boat heading across the wind (on a reach), with the sail out about halfway (Fig. 16), the wind tries to push the boat sideways. The centerboard prevents this, and the boat is forced to move ahead. It is literally "squeezed" along by the wind. This squeezing effect is explained in Figure 20.

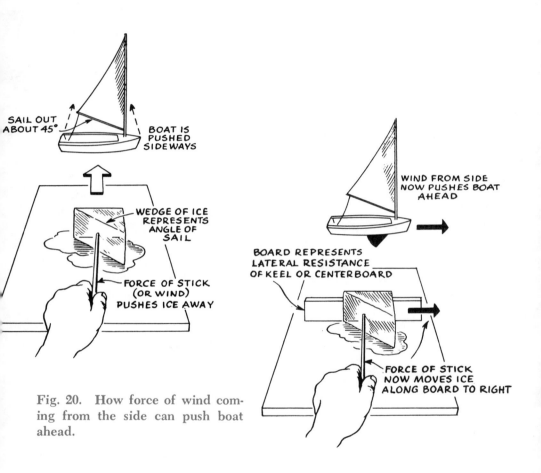

SAIL OUT ABOUT 45°

BOAT IS PUSHED SIDEWAYS

WEDGE OF ICE REPRESENTS ANGLE OF SAIL

FORCE OF STICK (OR WIND) PUSHES ICE AWAY

WIND FROM SIDE NOW PUSHES BOAT AHEAD

BOARD REPRESENTS LATERAL RESISTANCE OF KEEL OR CENTERBOARD

FORCE OF STICK NOW MOVES ICE ALONG BOARD TO RIGHT

Fig. 20. How force of wind coming from the side can push boat ahead.

3. How a boat sails "into" the wind. When a sailboat heads so that its bow makes an angle of 45 degrees to the wind direction, it is *beating,* or *on a beat* (Fig. 21). Here the sail is pulled in *(trimmed)* so that the boom is over the rear corner of the boat (the *after corner,* or *quarter*).

SAIL IS TRIMMED IN SO BOOM IS OVER CORNER OF DECK

BOARD REPRESENTS KEEL OR CENTERBOARD

NARROWER WEDGE OF ICE REPRESENTS SAIL TRIMMED IN CLOSE

45°

BOAT MOVES AHEAD AT 45° ANGLE WITH WIND

Fig. 21.

45°

FORCE OF STICK (WIND) "SQUEEZES" ICE FORWARD

Figure 21 shows how the boat is able to sail into the wind on a beat. Again, the wind has the same effect of "squeezing" the boat ahead.

4. A boat cannot sail closer into the wind than 45 degrees. When a boat heads so that it is pointing toward the wind at an angle less than about 45 degrees, the wind is able to strike the sail on both sides, and causes it to shake, or luff. When the sail luffs, the power is gone and the boat stops (Fig. 22).

How can the wind strike both sides of the sail at the same time? This is because of the normal curve to the sail, as we shall see.

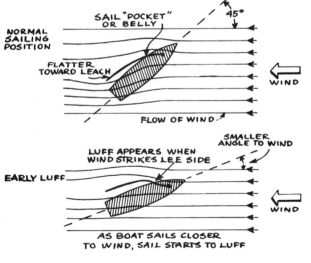

Fig. 22. As the boat heads closer to the wind than 45°, the pocket of the sail is struck by the wind on both sides, and the sail luffs.

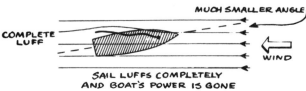

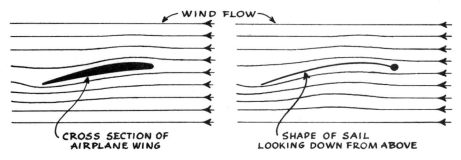

CROSS SECTION OF
AIRPLANE WING

SHAPE OF SAIL
LOOKING DOWN FROM ABOVE

Fig. 23.   The airfoil shape of the sail is similar to an airplane wing.

5. Airfoil shape of the sail. Sails are sewn together from patterns so that instead of being perfectly flat, they have a gentle curve to them when the wind blows. If we look down on the sail from above the mast, we see that this curve is like the top of an airplane wing (Fig. 23).

This is called an airfoil shape, and allows the sail to go through the wind smoothly and with more driving power than a flat sail. (The reasons for this are too complicated to discuss here, and are taken up in Chapter 10.)

The deeper part of the curve, near the mast, is sometimes called the "belly" or "pocket" of the sail. It extends about one third of the way back from the mast. The rest of the sail is flatter. As a result, as the boat heads closer into the wind (so the bow points more directly to the source of wind), the pocket is struck by wind on the opposite side (Fig. 22), and the sail luffs.

Luffing, then, is the shaking of the sail, starting in the deep part of the sail's curve near the mast. It occurs when the sail is headed too close into the wind.

6. The sailing directions and their names: (Fig. 24)

Fig. 24.

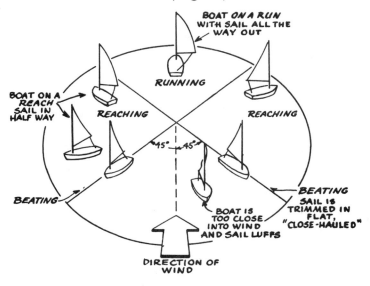

BOAT ON A RUN
WITH SAIL ALL THE
WAY OUT

RUNNING

BOAT ON A
REACH
SAIL IN
HALF WAY

REACHING

REACHING

45°   45°

BEATING

BEATING

BOAT IS
TOO CLOSE
INTO WIND
AND SAIL LUFFS

BEATING
SAIL IS
TRIMMED IN
FLAT,
"CLOSE-HAULED"

DIRECTION OF
WIND

THE THREE BASIC FACTORS IN SAILING

We have learned the theory of what makes a sailboat go. Sailing depends on three simple things:

(1) Direction of the wind

(2) Heading of the boat

(3) Trim of the sails

If we know and understand each one of these things and put them all together, we can make the wind work for us. Our sailboat will go properly and safely. Every good sailor keeps these three factors constantly in mind. So should you.

Let us learn all about each one, starting with the most important, the wind.

7. Wind direction. Wind is the most important factor, because it supplies the power which moves us along. We know that we can only sail in certain directions in relation to the wind (beating, reaching or running). Thus, the wind direction also determines where we can head our boat and how we can trim our sails.

The direction of the wind is the direction the wind is coming from. For example, a north wind comes from the north and is blowing toward the south. An east wind comes from an easterly direction and is blowing to the west, etc.

On sailing diagrams the wind is shown by an arrow, which flies *with the wind* (Fig. 25).

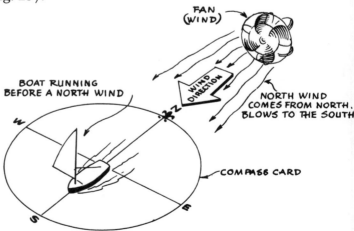

Fig. 25. Wind direction is where the wind comes from.

8. How to tell wind direction. There are many things on land and water that help the sailor find where the wind is coming from.

(a) Trees blowing in the wind. Leaves turn, and branches bend with the wind.

(b) Smoke from factory chimneys, or fires.

(c) Cat's paws. These are the dark ripples on the water that fresh wind makes. They move across the water with the direction of the wind.

(d) Flags on houses, boats, yacht clubs, etc. Also weather vanes.

(e) Boats at anchor. These will swing away from the wind, like weather vanes. But if there is a strong current or tide, the water may swing it around to head into the current. This is called a "tide lie."

(f) Pennants and telltales. These are small pieces of cloth ribbon or yarn which are attached to the shrouds or the masthead. They fly out with the wind. On a boat at anchor or not moving, they tell the *true wind* direction, and are useful. If the boat moves, they only show *apparent wind* direction (Fig. 26).

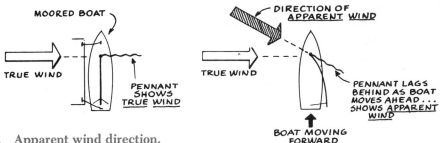

Fig. 26.   Apparent wind direction.

The *apparent wind* is that wind direction indicated by a telltale or wind pennant on a boat that is moving. As the boat moves ahead, the pennant seems to "drag" behind as it passes through the air. This changes its direction slightly and makes the wind appear to be coming from farther ahead than it really is.

(g) Wet finger. When held into the wind, a wet finger becomes cool on the side nearest the wind. On a warm day the side of your face nearest the wind will also feel cool and help show you wind direction.

(h) The luff of the sail. *This is by far the best method of knowing the wind direction.* You know that a boat can sail up to about a 45-degree angle into the wind. After this, the sail luffs. If you head

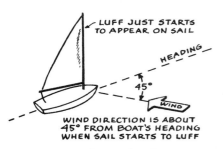

LUFF JUST STARTS
TO APPEAR ON SAIL

HEADING

45°

WIND

WIND DIRECTION IS ABOUT
45° FROM BOAT'S HEADING
WHEN SAIL STARTS TO LUFF

Fig. 27. Telling wind direction by
the luff of the sail.

your boat slowly up into the wind (Fig. 27) until the sail just begins
to luff (the first little flutter of sail near the mast), you will know
that the wind is just about 45 degrees off your bow.

Learn to use this method of finding the wind direction.

9. Heading of the boat with respect to the wind. The heading of a
boat is always the direction the bow points. It is the same as the
course steered.

It may be indicated by a compass direction, such as a northerly
course, or "heading north." We are interested in the boat's heading
with respect to the wind direction. This tells us if the boat is on a
reach, a run, or a beat.

(a) *Changes in heading.* Changes of direction are given with
respect to the wind. *Head up* means to point the bow nearer the
wind (Fig. 28) by changing the boat's course. *Fall off (head off)*
means to point the bow farther away from the wind by altering
course in the opposite direction.

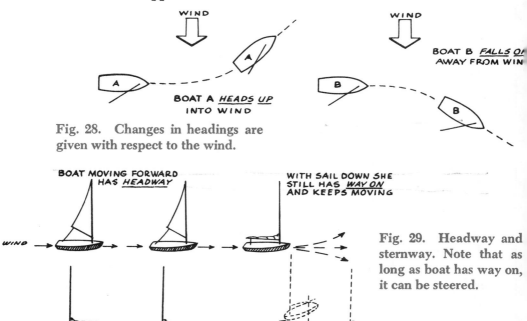

Fig. 28. Changes in headings are
given with respect to the wind.

Fig. 29. Headway and
sternway. Note that as
long as boat has way on,
it can be steered.

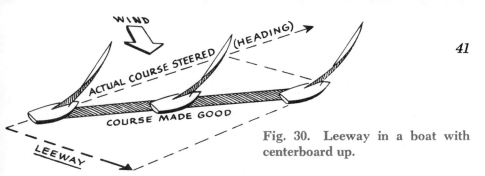

Fig. 30. Leeway in a boat with centerboard up.

(b) *Headway.* A boat moving in any direction is said to have "*way on.*" A drifting boat is "*under way.*" *Headway* is the forward motion of the boat (Fig. 29).

(c) *Sternway* is the backward motion of the boat. A boat may be steered if it has headway *or* sternway.

(d) *Leeway* is the sideways slippage of a boat in a direction away from the wind (Fig. 30). Because the hull beneath the water offers some lateral resistance, the boat moves slightly forward, too.

(e) *Normal leeway.* Almost every boat has some leeway. This is partly because the wind blows on the hull exposed above water, as well as on the sail (Fig. 31).

Fig. 31. Normal leeway in a boat with centerboard down.

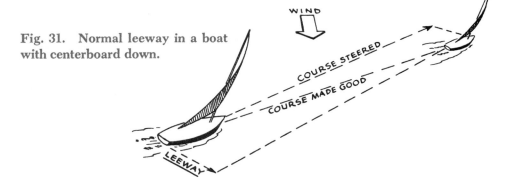

(f) The *course made good* is the actual line, if we could draw one on the water, over which the boat has sailed.

(g) The *track of disturbance.* As the boat moves through the water, it leaves waves and a wake. A line through the middle of the wake is called the *track,* or *track of disturbance.* It often corresponds to the course made good (Fig. 32).

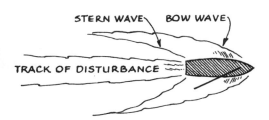

Fig. 32. Track of disturbance.

(h) *How to steer.* Most boats steer by means of a rudder, which is controlled by a handle or tiller. When the tiller is pushed to one side, the boat will turn to the opposite side. In other words, a sailboat steers as if the tiller were the handle of an outboard motor.

It is clear to see that as the tiller is moved to one side, the rudder swings to the other. This actually turns the stern of the boat first, and the whole boat seems to spin about a central *pivot point.*

(i) The *pivot point* is an imaginary point in the boat, usually near the centerboard well, about which the boat seems to turn (Fig. 33). It is roughly at the same point as the center of lateral resistance (Fig. 19).

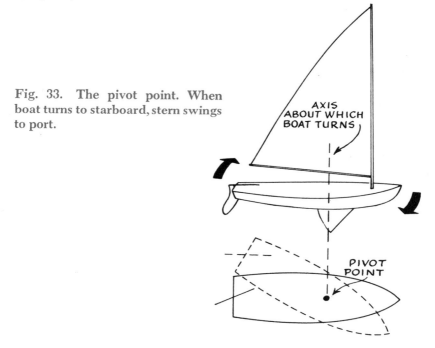

Fig. 33. The pivot point. When boat turns to starboard, stern swings to port.

10. Trim of sails with respect to wind. The position of your sail is always determined by where the wind is coming from (Fig. 34).

When the wind is behind (boat is running), the sail is out all the way. The boom makes a 90-degree or right angle to the boat. It is never let out farther than this.

When the wind is from the side, the sail is out about halfway. Figure 34 shows that on a *broad reach* the sail is farther out than on a *beam reach* or a *close reach.* But in each case, the sail's angle to the

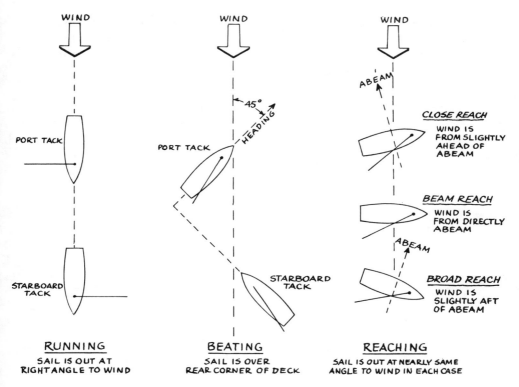

Fig. 34. The general trim of sails depends on heading and wind direction.

wind is nearly the same. This exact angle is determined by the point at which the sail luffs, and will be discussed in Chapter 3.

When the boat is beating (sailing *on the wind*), the sail is brought in so the boom is over the after corner of the deck. This is *close-hauled*. Trimming the sail any tighter does not work, and actually makes the boat slow down.

Terms for handling sails (remember, the *sheet* is the line which controls the boom and moves the sail in or out):

(a) *Ease the sheet, ease off, ease out.* All mean to let the sheet (and the sail) out.

(b) *Harden the sheet, harden in, haul in the sheet.* These mean to bring the sheet in, and *flatten sail*.

(c) To *start the sheet* is to slack off, or loosen.

11. Windward and leeward. Those objects closer to the wind are on the windward side of a boat, while those away from the wind are on the leeward (pronounced "loo-ard") side (Fig. 35). The general direction toward the wind is called *upwind,* while away from the wind is *downwind.* The boom is always over the leeward side.

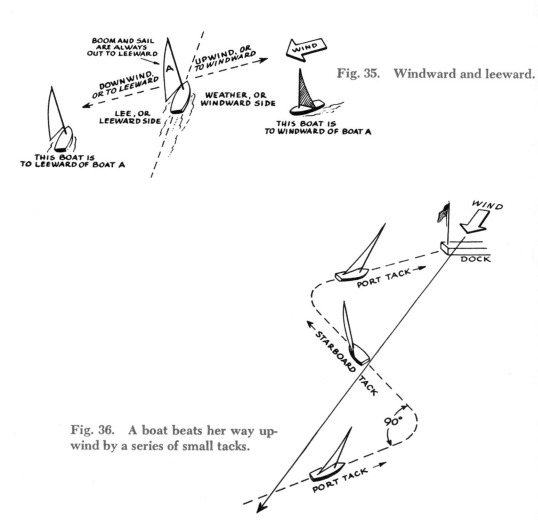

Fig. 35.   Windward and leeward.

Fig. 36.   A boat beats her way upwind by a series of small tacks.

12. How a boat moves upwind. Since a boat cannot sail directly into the wind, how can it get to a place that is near the direction the wind is coming from?

This is done by *coming about* frequently and taking a series of small *tacks* upwind (see Fig. 36).

13. Tacking, coming about and jibing. A *tack* is a name for a sailing course, and is determined by which side the sail is on.

A boat is on a *port tack* if the wind comes over the port side first to reach the sail. It is on *starboard tack* if the wind crosses the starboard side first.

Another way to remember it is that the tack is named for the side opposite the one the boom is over. If the boom is out to starboard, the boat is on a port tack. (See Fig. 37.) If boom is to port, it is a starboard tack.

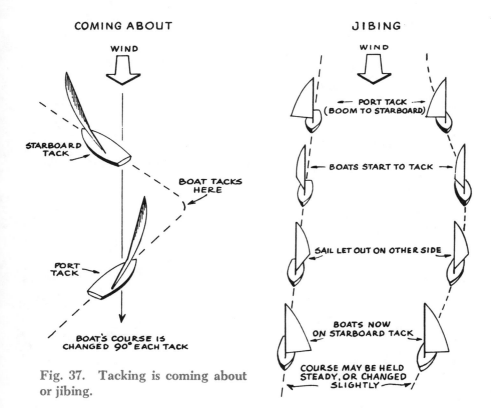

COMING ABOUT   JIBING

Fig. 37. Tacking is coming about or jibing.

Tacking means changing the sail from one side of the boat to the other. This can be done when the boat is headed *downwind* or *upwind,* but not across the wind.

Coming about is changing to the opposite tack while beating into the wind.

Jibing is changing to the opposite tack while running downwind.

BASIC KNOTS AND SEAMANSHIP

The square knot. (Fig. 38)

Use: For joining small lines of equal size, reefing sail, tying lashings, tying in battens.

Not used: Where there is a great deal of pull on the line, because knot will tighten and be very difficult to untie.

Step 1: Hold one rope in each hand. Now cross left over right, and

Step 2: . . . right over left. The knot has a "square" look to it.

Fig. 38.   The square knot.

The figure-8 knot. (Fig. 39)

Use: End of sheets, to keep them from running through blocks; end of life lines. Can be taken out very easily.

Step 1: Twist line into loop, near end.
Step 2: Put end through loop and pull tight.

Fig. 39.   The figure-8 knot.

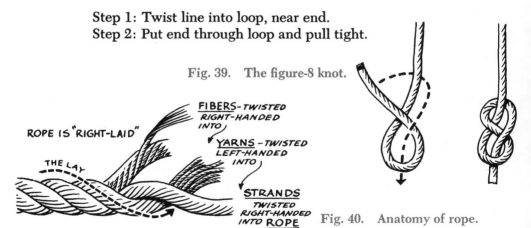

ROPE IS "RIGHT-LAID"

THE LAY

FIBERS—*TWISTED RIGHT-HANDED INTO*

YARNS—*TWISTED LEFT-HANDED INTO*

STRANDS *TWISTED RIGHT-HANDED INTO* ROPE

Fig. 40.   Anatomy of rope.

Parts of rope. When rope is used aboard a boat, it is called "line." We speak of the anchor line, the bow line, etc.

Rope may be made of nylon, Dacron, linen, and cotton, etc., but the commonest is hemp fiber. The *fibers* are rolled into *yarns*, the yarns are twisted into *strands*, and these are made into *rope*. The direction the strand lines run is called the *lay* (Fig. 40).

EXERCISES

QUESTIONS

1. Tell whether the boats described below are beating, reaching, or running.
    (a) Sail is out at right angle (90 degrees) to wind.
    (b) Centerboard has to be down.
    (c) Boat is sailing with wind abeam.
    (d) Sail makes a 45-degree angle with the wind.
    (e) Centerboard may be up or down.
    (f) Boat is sailing in same direction as the wind.
    (g) Sail makes about a 45-degree angle with the boat.
2. The resistance of a boat to moving sideways in the water is called _____ . In small boats this is provided mainly by the _____ , but also by the _____ and the _____ .
3. You are sailing across the wind on a reach. What happens to your direction or course when the centerboard is raised, and why?
4. Multiple choice. Choose the correct answer:
    (a) The best indicator of wind direction is (the telltales, the directions in which birds are being blown, the luff of the sail).
    (b) A boat moving backward has (leeway, backway, sternway).
    (c) Leeway can be corrected by moving the centerboard (up, down, toward the stern).
    (d) Pushing the tiller to the port side (moves the bow to starboard, moves bow to port, moves stern to starboard).
    (e) When a sailboat turns, it seems to pivot around (the bow, the stern, some point near the middle).
5. Why can't a boat sail into the wind much closer than 45 degrees?
6. What are the three basic factors in sailing a boat?
7. The luff of the sail is the best way to find wind direction. Explain how it is done.
8. List five other things that will help you find direction of the wind.
9. Answer true or false:
    (a) _____ A boat's heading means where it is coming from.
    (b) _____ A north wind blows toward the north.
    (c) _____ To head up means to point the bow nearer the wind.
    (d) _____ "Fall off" is what skipper calls when he wants boat to slow down.
    (e) _____ A boat moving forward has headway, is underway, and has way on.
    (f) _____ Beating is tacking upwind.
    (g) _____ *Ease the sheet* and *start the sheet* mean the same.
    (h) _____ The pivot point and center of lateral resistance are usually at or near the same place.
    (i) _____ The pivot point is the same thing as the center of lateral resistance.

48

(j)_____The boat's heading is always the same as the course made good.

10. Write a short definition of these terms:
   (a) Close-hauled
   (b) Start the sheet
   (c) Leeward
   (d) Windward
   (e) Jibing
   (f) Coming about
   (g) Leeward side
   (h) Heading up
   (i) Port tack
   (j) Starboard tack

PRACTICE DRILL

1. Learn your fundamentals first. If you are not in a formal sailing class, purchase one or two small model boats and borrow the use of a small electric fan. If the boat has two sails, remove the jib for now. Remove any metal keel so the boat will rest upright on a table (it may tilt slightly). The mainsail should have a sheet that runs through a small eye and fastens to a nail or cleat. Use the model and fan in the following lessons.

2. Start with fan on and the model boat pointing directly into the wind. This shows the sail luffing. Turn the boat at a 45-degree angle to wind, then trim sail in close-hauled and notice that luffing stops. Hold the sheet in your hand and turn the boat away from the wind (falling off), while gradually letting out the sail until the model is running before the wind. Continue around, trimming in sail as the boat heads up.

3. With a piece of chalk, draw on the table the various wind directions for a boat under sail (beating, reaching, running). Put your boat in the center and notice the proper sail trim in each of these quadrants.

4. With the fan on, draw an arrow toward your boat to show the wind direction. Set the sail close-hauled. Now move the fan to a new position and watch what happens to the boat. Try to see whether the sail should be let out or the boat's position changed for this wind shift. Then go on to Chapter 3, where this will be fully discussed.

5. Review Chapter 1 on getting the boat ready for sailing and on basic principles in launching and mooring boat.

6. If you have had a little experience or have a friend or instructor who knows some sailing and can go with you, take your boat out in some light wind. DO NOT GO FAR FROM SHORE OR PIER, but practice sailing principles. Sail on a beat, a reach, and a run, and try to trim the sail as shown in Figure 34. Raise the centerboard when reaching or beating and look behind you to see how this gives you leeway.

3. Sailing to Windward

1. Review. Before setting out in a boat, let us review the steps we have learned thus far.

In Chapter 1 we learned how to rig the boat and put up the sail. We learned that when the boat is in the water, the centerboard is lowered first for stability. Also, the boat is headed directly into the wind whenever sail is hoisted or lowered, and headed into the wind when landing. These rules must be kept in mind at all times.

In Chapter 2 we learned the three basic factors of sailing: (1) direction of the wind, (2) heading of the boat, and (3) trim of the sails in relation to the wind.

Now let's get into a boat, hoist sail and shove off . . . and see if we can put all of these things together.

2. Sailing to windward. In this chapter we will discuss the problems in sailing to windward. Sailing to windward means being on any heading where the front (bow) of the boat is more into the wind than away from it.

Sailing on a beam reach is the dividing line between sailing to windward or to leeward. If the boat on a beam reach heads up, it is sailing to windward. If it falls off, it is sailing to leeward. The problems of sail and boat handling are different in each case.

As we shove off in our boat to windward, we have a choice of two things. We can set our course — for example, to a dock or point on the other shore — and then trim our sail in or out for this heading.

Or, we can trim the sail in close-hauled, and then beat up to windward on whatever course the wind allows us.

3. Set your course, then adjust the sail. Once you know the wind direction, set the course you want to steer. Find some object on shore and point toward it. In sailing to windward, this means you will be on a beat, or somewhere on a close reach (Fig. 41).

Keep your course steady. Now, trim the sail. This is done by letting out the sheet (and sail) *slowly*, until the sail begins to luff near the mast. Then stop letting out the sheet. Begin to bring it in slowly, until the luff in the sail just disappears.

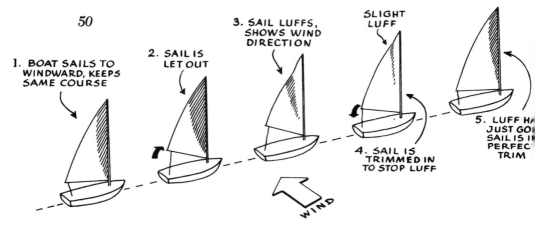

Fig. 41.   Sailing on a steady course, sail is brought in until it just stops luffing.

This gives you the perfect trim of sail for the heading you have chosen, and gives the sail maximum power. This method of trimming sail is always used whenever the boat's course is steady. Know it.

SUMMARY OF STEPS IN ADJUSTING SAIL:
(1) Find wind direction.
(2) Choose a course (close reach or beat), and stay on same course, or heading.
(3) Let sail out until it starts to luff.
(4) Trim sail in until the luff *just* stops.

4. Trim your sail, then adjust your heading. This method does just the opposite. The sail is trimmed first and the heading found to suit it (Fig. 42).

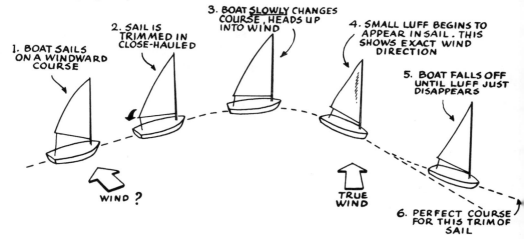

Fig. 42.   With sail trimmed first, boat rounds up until sail starts to luff, then falls off.

First find the wind direction. Sail a general course to windward (anywhere on a close reach or beat). Trim your sail close-hauled, or wherever you want it, and keep it there. With the sail fixed in position, let your boat head up slowly into the wind. This is done by pushing the tiller over toward the leeward side.

Watch the sail near the mast for a luff. When the first flutter in the sail appears, head the boat slowly away from the wind just enough so the luff disappears. This is the proper heading for the trim of your sail.

SUMMARY OF STEPS IN FINDING HEADING:

(1) Find wind direction.
(2) Trim sail to a fixed position (such as close-hauled) and keep it there.
(3) Head boat slowly up into wind until sail starts to luff.
(4) Fall off until luff just stops. Keep this course.

5. Beating. In sailing on a beat you try to combine both methods. First find the wind direction and sail in the general direction of a beat (about 45 degrees off the wind). Trim the sail close-hauled and head up slowly into the wind. When you see the luff first appear in the sail, fall off slightly *or* trim the sail in a little bit tighter. Usually you will do both. But don't bring the boom in much farther than the after corner of your deck. This flattens the sail too much and the boat loses its forward power.

6. Wind changes. What happens if the wind comes from a new direction while you are sailing? Most winds shift direction (or *haul*) a few degrees quite frequently during the day. You usually cannot tell these shifts by your wind pennant or telltales, but you can tell by the sails. The luff of your sail is the best and most important wind indicator you have (Fig. 43).

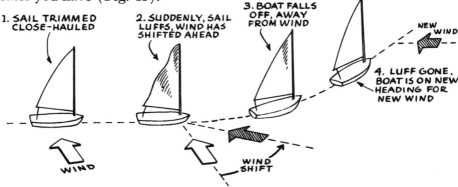

Fig. 43. Luff in sail shows that wind has shifted more ahead, and boat falls off to new heading.

If the wind changes so that it is more ahead of you, the sail will luff (Fig. 43). This is because the angle of your heading into the wind is now less than 45 degrees. To correct this, fall off away from the wind until the sail fills again and the luff stops. This is your new heading.

What happens if the wind shifts the other way? Now there is no new luff in the sail to tell you the wind has changed (Fig. 44). If you keep on the same course, the wind may shift dead abeam without your knowing it. The wind blows at nearly right angles to your sail and most of the sail's power is lost.

To prevent this, you must "test the wind" constantly. This means heading up *slowly* into the wind until the sail begins to luff. If the wind remains in the same direction, you will luff at once. Then you fall off and resume your course.

If the sail doesn't luff, keep heading up slowly until it does. This tells you the new wind direction and what your new course will be (Fig. 44).

When on a beat, this is the only way you can tell when the wind has shifted abeam. Therefore, learn to test the wind frequently while beating.

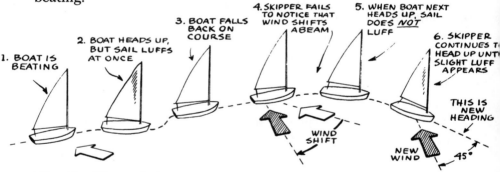

Fig. 44. "Testing" the wind by heading up shows that wind has shifted more abeam.

SUMMARY

HOW TO SAIL ON A BEAT:

(1) Trim the sheet close-hauled, and

(2) Head up into wind slowly until sail luffs.

(3) Fall off until luff stops. This is your course for beating.

HOW TO TELL WIND SHIFTS:

(1) If sail luffs, wind has shifted ahead. Fall off.

(2) If sail does not luff, ease up into wind until it does. This is new course.

7. Pointing and footing. *Pointing* is a boat's ability to sail close to the wind. A boat on a beat points higher (into the wind) than a boat on a reach. *Footing* refers to the boat's speed over the water. If one boat foots faster than (or outfoots) another, its speed is greater (Fig. 45).

When beating, you try to point as high as possible, and yet foot as fast as possible. By trimming sheets so the boom is in nearly over the center of the cockpit, you can sometimes point higher than 45 degrees. This is called *pinching*. However, when you pinch you lose speed and will drop behind other boats if you are racing.

Every boat has a different ability to point or foot. It is just the way they are built. It is up to you to find out what your boat can do best.

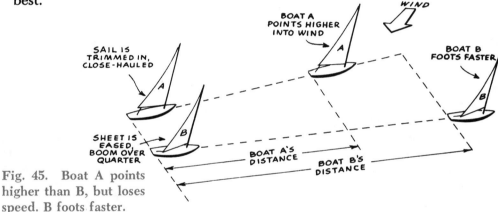

Fig. 45. Boat A points higher than B, but loses speed. B foots faster.

HERE ARE SOME TIPS ON BEATING:

(1) Make all changes in heading very slowly. Ease the tiller gradually over to leeward when heading upwind.

(2) If boat seems too slow, try falling off. You may be pointing too high.

(3) If this doesn't work, slack sheets a bit. Pinching will also slow the boat.

(4) Constantly watch the sail just behind the mast. This is where the luff appears first.

(5) Steer by watching the luff of your mainsail, not the telltales. The luff tells you the wind direction at once.

(6) Keep easing up to windward to test the wind for any new shift.

8. Coming about. (Fig. 46). In beating to windward, it is often necessary to change tacks. This is called *coming about,* and is done by turning the bow into the wind and continuing around until the sail fills on the other side. Here is how it is done:

(a) *The boat must be beating and the sails close-hauled.* If sail is out, trim in. If sailing on a reach, head up to a beating course first.

(b) *Skipper gives commands to crew.* First he says, "Stand by to come about." This means he and crew are ready, but no one moves yet. It is a preparatory command, and warns of what is going to happen.

Next he says, "Hard alee." This is a command of execution, and the maneuver starts. Now everyone moves. The skipper pushes the

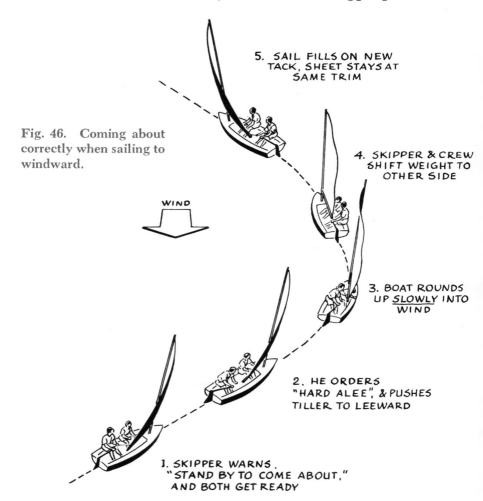

Fig. 46.   Coming about correctly when sailing to windward.

5. SAIL FILLS ON NEW TACK, SHEET STAYS AT SAME TRIM

4. SKIPPER & CREW SHIFT WEIGHT TO OTHER SIDE

WIND

3. BOAT ROUNDS UP <u>SLOWLY</u> INTO WIND

2. HE ORDERS "HARD ALEE", & PUSHES TILLER TO LEEWARD

1. SKIPPER WARNS. "STAND BY TO COME ABOUT," AND BOTH GET READY

tiller to the lee side of the boat and the bow starts to round up into the wind. These commands are always given when coming about in order to prevent confusion in the boat.

(c) *Skipper's duties.* The skipper is in charge and does the steering. He moves the tiller to the lee side, then controls it so the boat heads up fairly fast into the wind and falls off on the other tack. But not too far. The new tack should be at a right angle (90 degrees) to the old, so you know about where your new heading will be before you come about.

Here's a tip on how to find your new heading before you come about. Look directly across the side of your boat (dead abeam). Find a landmark such as a tree or house on the other shore. When you come about your new course will be heading right for your landmark (Fig. 47).

Fig. 47. By sighting at an object dead abeam, skipper can tell where new course will be.

(d) *Crew's duties.* When the skipper says "Hard alee," the crew starts to move to the opposite side of the boat, ducking under the boom as it swings by. He does not adjust the mainsheet or sail, since the sail will be trimmed just the same on the new tack.

(e) *Shifting weight.* Since the wind blowing on the sail tends to tip the boat over toward the leeward side, both skipper and crew usually sit on the windward side to balance it. As you come about, both skipper and crew shift their weight to the other side.

What about shifting position forward or backward in the boat? This is called fore-and-aft trim of the hull, and will be discussed in a later chapter. In general, it is best to sit near the center, as close to the pivot point as possible, rather than far out in the bow or stern. This helps the boat turn faster.

SUMMARY ON HOW TO COME ABOUT:

(1) Be sure you are close-hauled and on a beat.
(2) Give preparatory command, "Stand by to come about," to warn crew.
(3) Say, "Hard alee," when you start to tack, and push tiller to lee side.
(4) Let boat round up into wind and then fall off on new tack, at right angles (90 degrees) to old.
(5) Do not change trim of sail.

9. In irons. (Fig. 48). What happens if your boat heads up into the wind and can't get around? If it loses headway, or momentum, it is said to be *in irons* or *in stays*. A boat in irons is helpless. The sail is luffing. The boat is dead in the water, without headway. It cannot be steered. It is at the mercy of the wind. Sometimes the skipper must get out a paddle and turn the boat around. But there is another way.

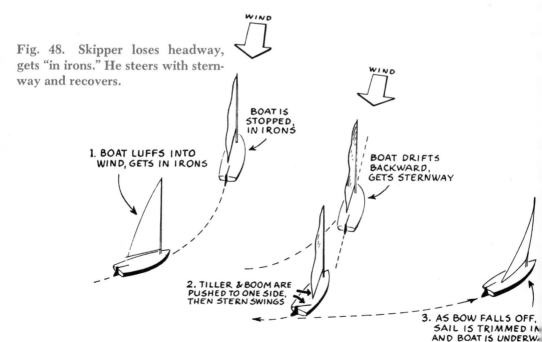

Fig. 48. Skipper loses headway, gets "in irons." He steers with sternway and recovers.

Although the boat in irons is not moving, the wind blowing on it soon starts it backward, giving it sternway. Now all you have to do is push both tiller and boom hard over to one side. Since you have sternway, you are "steering backward," and the stern will swing to the opposite side. The boat is now across the wind, not heading into it. The wind fills the sail, and you are off again.

10. Sailing on a reach. When you are sailing a reaching course you have already chosen the boat's heading. To trim the sail properly, let it out until it luffs, then trim in until the luff just disappears. This is the same method discussed in Section 3 and shown in Figure 41.

To find wind changes, the sail must be eased out frequently. As you see the luff appear near the mast, trim in. The sail acts like a weather vane, shows you where the wind is, and should always be trimmed to the angle where the luff just disappears.

11. Tacking from a reach. Tacking means the changing of the boom from one side of the boat to the other (and the sail filling from the other side). You must never try to do it while reaching! If you wish to tack by coming about into the wind, you must round up to a beating course first and trim in the sail close-hauled.

If you don't, you will lose speed and headway in trying to go the longer distance of the turn. The sail will luff before you are headed into the wind, since it is already out a good way from the boat.

SUMMARY OF SAILING ON A REACH:
(1) Keep on steady course.
(2) Let sail out until it luffs. Trim in until luff just stops.
(3) Ease sail out frequently to test for wind shifts.
(4) Don't tack from a reach. Head up to a beating course and close-haul sails first.

BASIC KNOTS AND SEAMANSHIP

The round turn and two half hitches. (Fig. 49)

Use: For mooring boat to dock or piling, fastening anchor line to anchor, tying towline to mast, etc.

The round turn reduces amount of chafing and wearing on rope. If there is a heavy pull, add extra turns.

Step 1: Take two round turns (or more) around post.

Step 2: Make first half hitch, and keep going around line in same direction for second half hitch.

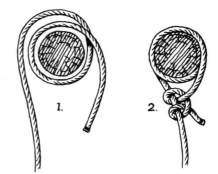

Fig. 49. Round turn and two half hitches.

The clove hitch. (Fig. 50)

Use: Tying line to any round piling or post, but not for heavy pulling. Good for temporary moorings.

Step 1: Form an underhand loop and drop over post.

Step 2: Form second underhand loop just like the first, and drop over post also.

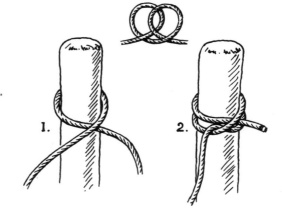

Fig. 50. The clove hitch.

EXERCISES

QUESTIONS

1. Write a brief definition for each of these terms:
    (a) Sailing to windward
    (b) Wind shift
    (c) Pointing
    (d) Hard alee
    (e) "In irons"
2. Good skippers will tell you that when beating, you should "sail by your luff." What does this mean?
3. You want to sail on a beat, with sail close-hauled. List the four general steps you would take to do this.
4. If your sail begins to luff while beating, which way has the wind shifted (further ahead, or further back)? How do you test the wind for wind shifts?
5. Multiple choice. Choose the best single answer:
    (a) When the boom is trimmed in over the middle of the cockpit, the boat can sometimes point higher than 45 degrees into the wind, but usually goes slower. This is called (pointing, pinching, footing, beating).
    (b) If the boat seems too slow while beating, try (heading up higher, easing sheet, hardening sheet).
    (c) Test the wind on a beat by (falling off slowly, heading up slowly, letting sail out) if luff doesn't appear.
    (d) The luff in the sail appears first (along the foot, at the leach, near the mast).
6. You are coming about. Select the steps from column B and put them in the proper order in column A.

A	B
(1) _____	(a) "Hard alee"
	(b) "Ready about" or "Stand by to come about"
(2) _____	
	(c) Skipper changes from a reach to a beat
(3) _____	
	(d) Skipper pushes tiller to same side of boat boom is on
(4) _____	
	(e) Skipper pushes tiller to opposite side of boat boom is on
(5) _____	
	(f) Crew ducks under boom

7. How do you get out of irons?
8. Answer true or false:
    (a) _____ A boat can tack easily from a reach.
    (b) _____ When reaching, easing sheet out frequently is a good idea.
    (c) _____ When reaching, a luff is kept in the sail at all times.

(d) _____ Wind shifts are harder to discover when reaching than when beating.

(e) _____ In general, it is best to sit near the centerboard well in a small boat.

(f) _____ If skipper can sit far in the stern and rest his back, boat will come about more easily.

(g) _____ When tacking, the new course will be at right angles to the old.

(h) _____ Crew lets the sheet out as boat heads up to come about.

(i) _____ A flutter in the sail along the leach means the wind has probably shifted.

(j) _____ When sailing on a steady course, sail is brought in only until it stops luffing, no further.

PRACTICE DRILL

1. Before you set sail, find the direction of the wind and be sure you remember it. Now find some object or point in the water around which you can sail a reaching course from your dock and back.

2. Sail on a reach toward this point or marker, and be sure you go around it heading into the wind. As you approach your dock, head up into the wind and practice making a landing. At this point you should be headed directly into the wind with the sail luffing. Shove off and try again. Switch with crew. When on the reach, trim sails by the luff, as taught. But be sure to trim in at the mark and sail on a beat before tacking.

3. Repeat this drill over and over until you can land your boat at the dock perfectly — no bumping, little or no way on, and with sail luffing.

4. Practice steering. Sail on a long reach, by looking at some object up ahead toward which you can steer. Occasionally look behind at your wake. Is your track of disturbance a straight line? It should be. Try sailing a straight course by looking at the water up ahead.

5. Practice maneuvering. Now try beating, but don't go out if the wind is too strong unless you have read Chapter 5 on water safety. Have crew trim sail close-hauled, then round up slowly to a beat. Try to steer a course by *watching the luff of your sail only*. After sailing a short while, look behind at your track of disturbance and see what kind of course you steered. If you had a lot of leeway and were slipping off to the side, you forgot to put your centerboard down.

6. Try coming about. Take turns with crew handling tiller and sheet. Before each come about, have a contest with the crew to see who can guess closest where next tack will head you (see Fig. 47).

4. Sailing to Leeward

1. Review. In the previous chapters we learned the three basic factors in sailing: wind direction, boat heading, and trim of sail. By combining these we were able to sail to windward. We set our course and adjusted the sail . . . or, we trimmed the sail and found the best course.

In sailing to leeward, the three basic factors are the same, but are harder to use. The wind is always coming from somewhere behind you and is hard to spill. On a broad reach you may be able to luff the sail by letting it out. But when sailing on a run, the boom can only go out 90 degrees to one side (it is stopped by the shrouds), and the sail cannot be made to luff.

This means that you will have more difficulty telling when the wind changes direction, since there is no luff in the sail to help you. Here it pays to watch your telltales.

However, sailing on a run is one of the nicest parts of sailing. You are running with the wind, the waves are behind you, the boat is level, and it is very restful. Sailors often call this the "downhill slide." But if you are out for a day's sail, don't start off on a run. The wind may drop and you may have a long time beating back home. Start out on a beat. It is harder work, but then you can rest on the run, and you can usually get home even if the wind drops greatly in force.

2. Sailing on a broad reach. The wind is coming from the side and from behind the beam, but not dead astern.

Sail adjustment. Just as on a close reach or beam reach, the course is already determined and the sail is trimmed in just beyond the point of luffing. Again, the sail must be let out almost continuously to test for wind shifts. (Fig. 51).

What happens if you let it out and it doesn't luff? If the boom is out at right angles (90 degrees) and the sail is full, you are *on a run*.

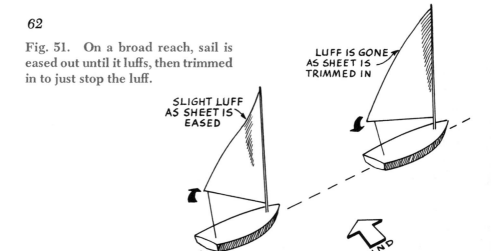

Fig. 51. On a broad reach, sail is eased out until it luffs, then trimmed in to just stop the luff.

Shifting weight. The wind does not tend to tip the boat as much on a broad reach, so the crew and skipper can sit more inboard. However, it is important to keep the boat level, as it will skim over the water faster than when heeling.

Centerboard. On a broad reach most boats go a little faster with the board about halfway up. This lessens the drag of the board through the water.

To adjust the board, pull it up part way. Look aft at your wake. If the boat seems to be slipping sideways through the water, lower the board. If the boat does not seem to be slipping much, raise the board a bit more. But *don't forget to lower it* when you change course and head up to a beat or close reach. Otherwise you will merely slip sideways downwind.

3. Sailing on a run. Here the wind is dead behind (astern), or nearly so. It may be one or two points off the quarter. Sail is out to one side, wind and waves are behind, and the boat does all the work. It looks easy and it is easy. But there is one big thing to watch out for: a wind shift and an *accidental jibe.* When this happens, the sail may be swung suddenly to the opposite side without warning. This is when most new sailors tip over. It will pay you to watch carefully for wind shifts.

Wind pennants and telltales. When sailing on a run, your wind indicators will show shifts before the sails do. This is the best time to keep a close eye on them.

Centerboard. In moderate winds you may pull it up when running, thus reducing drag through the water and letting the boat sail faster. However, in choppy or rough water, or if the boat tends to roll from side to side in waves, you should lower the board. This stabilizes the boat. There is very little forward resistance to the thin centerboard, anyway. When first learning to sail, leave your centerboard down.

Sailing by the lee. When you are running before the wind and find that it is coming over the same side of your boat that the sail is on, you are "sailing by the lee."

This is a dangerous thing to do (Fig. 52) because it means the wind is coming more from the lee side than astern and more likely to get behind the sail and jibe it. Watch the sail carefully aloft (the upper part). If there is any flutter or "soft spot," a part of the sail that is not pushed out in a nice curve by the wind, chances are you are *sailing by the lee* . . . and should jibe, or alter course, to be headed more downwind.

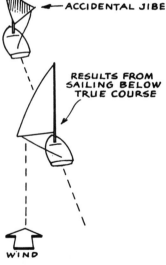

Fig. 52. On a run, sailing by the lee may lead to an accidental jibe.

4. Jibing. Jibing is changing tacks when sailing downwind. It is done by bringing the sail in on one side and letting it out on the other, without altering course appreciably.

If the wind catches the sail and snaps it across rapidly, the bottom half first — which raises the boom and tangles the sheet — it is called a *goose-wing jibe*. This type of jibe is dangerous. It can break your mast, knock you overboard, or capsize the boat. An accidental jibe like this can be prevented by keeping the sheet tight and *controlling the sail,* and by altering course whenever necessary to *keep the wind dead astern.*

How to jibe safely. More sailors get into trouble when trying to jibe than at any other time. It is a safe procedure if you learn to do it properly. It is *not* done by merely grabbing the boom, pulling it across the boat and throwing it out on the other side. This lets the sheet go slack where it will catch on fittings, and the sail is not controlled. Jibing is done correctly this way (Fig. 53).

(a) *Make sure wind is dead astern.* Look at your sail and see that it is full and without any luff or soft spots. Check the wind pennant and telltales. Alter course so they are streaming in front of you

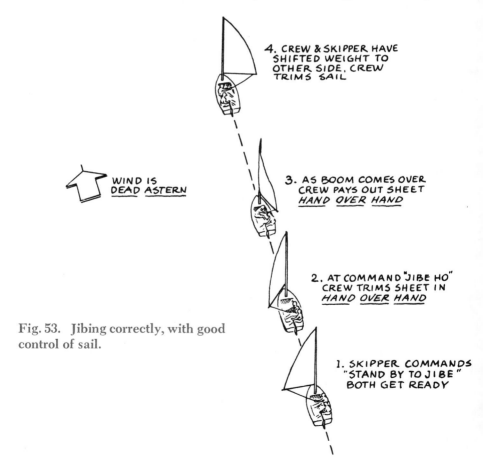

4. CREW & SKIPPER HAVE SHIFTED WEIGHT TO OTHER SIDE. CREW TRIMS SAIL

WIND IS DEAD ASTERN

3. AS BOOM COMES OVER CREW PAYS OUT SHEET *HAND OVER HAND*

2. AT COMMAND "JIBE HO" CREW TRIMS SHEET IN *HAND OVER HAND*

Fig. 53. Jibing correctly, with good control of sail.

1. SKIPPER COMMANDS "STAND BY TO JIBE" BOTH GET READY

(and the wind is directly behind). Only when you are running directly downwind is it safe to jibe.

(b) *Skipper commands, "Stand by to jibe."* No one moves, as this is a preparatory command warning crew that the next maneuver will be a jibe.

(c) *Skipper commands, "Jibe ho!"* When everyone is ready, skipper gives this command of execution, and the jibe starts. Skipper holds the tiller steady and sails a straight course. But you may alter course *a few degrees* toward the new windward side to make certain the wind doesn't cause an accidental jibe.

(d) *Duties of crew.* At the command "Jibe ho!" your crew begins to pull in the mainsheet *hand over hand.* When the boom is midway across the boat, the wind will catch the sail. Now your crew pays out the sheet rapidly, again hand over hand. In this way the sail is controlled, there is no sudden snap of the sail by the wind, and no *fouled sheet* (tangled, or caught on a fitting or the tiller, etc.).

If you are sailing alone, as many skippers do in very small boats, you can hold the tiller steady between your knees or by pushing your back against it. This leaves both hands free to haul on the sheet.

When the boom comes across, keep your head down and be ready to shift your weight to the other side of the boat (new windward side), should a sudden gust of wind catch your sail during the jibe.

SUMMARY ON HOW TO JIBE SAFELY:
(1) Make sure you are running and that wind is dead astern.
(2) Warn crew by commanding, "Stand by to jibe."
(3) Say "Jibe ho!" when you want jibe to start. Keep course steady, or head a few degrees to new windward side.
(4) Haul sheet in hand over hand, and pay out on other side.
(5) Shift weight to opposite side.

5. Basic sailing maneuvers and how to make them. You have learned how to sail on a beat, a reach, and a run. What happens when you go from one to the other? Here is an important rule: *Whenever you change course, for any reason, you must readjust the sail.*

For example, when sailing on a beat, your sail is close-hauled. On a run it is out at right angles to the boat. If you change course from a beat and fall off on a run, sail must be let out. But it also has to be adjusted in or out for every new heading, no matter how slight the change. In other words, whenever the skipper moves the tiller to change the course, the crew should be changing the trim of the sail. Remember this especially when changing from a beat to a reach or run. Let the sail out at once and then retrim.

Helpful hints. If you have changed course and don't know what to do with the sail, remember this:

(1) If sail is not luffing, let it out until it just does luff, then trim it in.

(2) If sail is already luffing, trim it in until it stops.

(3) If you let sail out all the way (90 degrees) and no luff appears, you are running downwind.

(4) If you trim in all the way (sail is close-hauled) and sail still luffs, you are heading too high into the wind. Fall off.

SUMMARY OF BASIC SAILING MANEUVERS:
(1) Whenever you change course, you must retrim sail either out or in to find the luff.
(2) Changing tacks when sailing to windward is called *coming about* or *tacking.*
(3) Changing tacks when sailing to leeward is called *jibing.*

6. Anchoring the small boat. On yachts larger than about 20 feet in length, anchors are always *lowered over the side,* not thrown. This is because the anchor is heavy and the line may catch in a fitting on deck and swing the anchor against the boat, causing much damage.

On small boats, if the anchor can be lifted easily with one hand, it can be heaved or tossed without danger. If it takes two hands to lift it, *lower it, don't toss it.*

Heaving the anchor. First, fasten one end of anchor line to the anchor and the other to the boat. Next, coil anchor rope neatly in left hand, with the coils which will come off first (nearest the anchor) at the finger tips. The skipper heads boat up into wind, sail luffs, boat slows and stops, then begins to gather sternway. This is the time to toss the anchor. Swing it underhand in an up-and-down direction (never sideways), and let it go. Open your left hand and let the coils of rope fall off as they are pulled out.

How much anchor line? As your boat gathers sternway, pay out the anchor line until you have at least four times the depth in length payed out. The length of anchor line is called *scope*, and should be four to seven times the depth of the water; otherwise the anchor won't hold. If the water is 5 feet deep, let out 20 to 35 feet of anchor line (Fig. 54).

Pass the anchor line through your bow chock, then secure to the cleat or bitt on the deck. If you are mooring for the night, take a turn around the mast for safekeeping. Remember, a change in wind or tide will swing your boat in a wide circle around the anchor, so check carefully and see that you are clear of docks and boats.

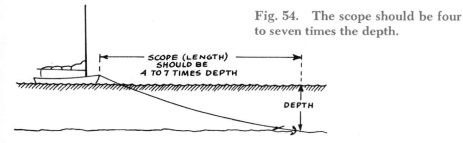

Fig. 54. The scope should be four to seven times the depth.

Mooring with a stern line or anchor. This is the most popular way of mooring a small boat, especially if there is tide or current. There are three good methods.

(a) *Temporary mooring.* On approaching a pier for a landing, drop the anchor on the way in. When the bow just touches the pier, make the anchor line fast at the stern. Now take a line from the bow and lead the boat farther up the pier or to the shore, where it can be tied so as not to hit the pier or other boats.

(b) *Continuous loop anchor line.* A second method is to put the boat on a kind of "pulley clothesline." Run a line from the pier to the ring on your anchor or to a block on the anchor ring (Fig. 55-A) and back to the boat. A second line runs from the bow of the boat to the

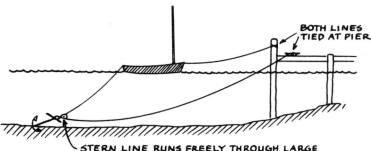

Fig. 55-A.

pier, and the boat is pulled in or let out as needed. The anchor can be dropped as before, or a buoy or permanent piling can be used (Fig. 55-B).

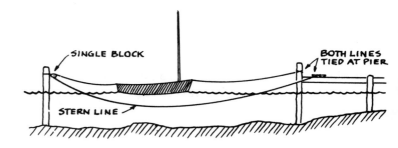

Fig. 55-B.

(c) *Weighted mooring.* A more permanent mooring can be made by using a pole, or piling, on which a weighted line is hung (Fig. 55-C). When the stern line is fastened to the boat, the weight will keep the bow away from the dock and still allow the boat to be pulled in to take on crew.

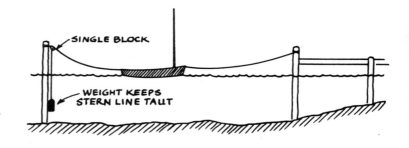

Fig. 55-C.

7. Leaving the crowded or windward dock. Leaving a dock or mooring is called *shoving off*. Sometimes when you are ready to shove off you will find boats crowded next to you, or that the wind has shifted against you, or other obstacles. Here a few simple tricks in seamanship are helpful.

Shoving off bow first. If the wind has shifted while you were tied up so it is now blowing toward the dock, simply turn your boat around to face the wind, hoist sail, and have a helper on the dock shove you by pushing hard on the *end of the boom*. This will give you enough headway to get clear until you are sailing on your own.

Shoving off stern first. If there were no other boats at the dock, you would normally push off your bow and leave the dock on a reach, crosswise to the wind. However, with boats on each side, this is not possible.

Here the best thing to do is have someone shove the boat directly backward. Keep your tiller in the middle while you gather sternway. When you are clear of other boats, put your tiller hard over to one side and let the stern swing. As soon as the boat is crosswise to the wind, trim the sail, pick up headway, and you are off! (Fig. 56).

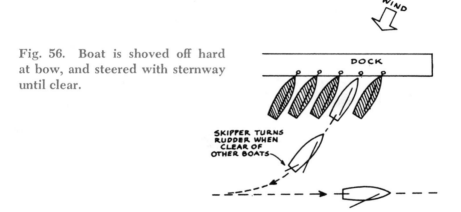

Fig. 56. Boat is shoved off hard at bow, and steered with sternway until clear.

Pulling off windward side of dock with anchor. If the wind is too strong and your boat too heavy to push off easily by the boom, it may be better to pull off with a small anchor.

The anchor may be dropped when mooring, or it may be taken out later in a small boat. Anchors under 20 pounds may be floated out by a swimmer using two life cushions or jackets tied together, with the anchor tied on top. Once the anchor is set, the bow is pulled around to head into the wind, sail is set, and when the boat gathers headway the anchor is brought up.

8. Tying boat at the dock. More damage results from careless tying of the boat to the dock than from anything except the big dramatic accident. First, try to secure your boat so it is not touching other boats. If it has to, tie a life jacket or cushion or fender between your boat and the next one, just at the point where the two boats will rub.

BASIC KNOTS AND SEAMANSHIP

The bowline (boe-l'n).

Use: One of your most important knots, the bowline, is used whenever a loop is needed that won't slip. It is used for mooring lines, seats, towlines, joining two ropes together, etc. It will always come out easily when strain is taken off line.

A. (Fig. 57)

Step 1: Make small loop near end, with shorter part crossing on top.

Step 2: Put end through loop, from underneath.

Step 3: Swing end around main part of line.

Step 4: Put end back through loop in same way it came out.

Fig. 57.   Forming the bowline as a free loop.

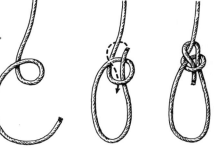

B. (Fig. 58)

Step 1: Throw line around post or spar, and form overhand knot.

Step 2: Snap the short end so it becomes a *straight line*. This should automatically make a loop in the other.

Step 3: Take short end out of this loop, around the main part, and back through the loop.

PULL
STRAIGHT

1

2

3

Fig. 58.   Forming the bowline around post or spar

EXERCISES

1. If you are out for a casual sail, it is better to start on a beat, rather than a run. Why?
2. What is sailing by the lee?
   Why is it dangerous?
3. Fill in the blanks:
   (a) When changing from a run to a reach or beat, the centerboard must be _____.
   (b) An accidental jibe may be prevented by keeping the boat headed _____.
   (c) As the jibe begins, crew can pull in on the _____.
4. You are sailing on a run, and are about to jibe. Choose the steps from column *B* and put them in proper order under *A*.

A	*B*
(1) _____	(a) "Stand by to jibe"
(2) _____	(b) "Jibe ho!"
(3) _____	(c) Crew pulls boom across from one side to other
(4) _____	(d) Skipper makes certain wind is directly behind
(5) _____	(e) Crew trims sheet in rapidly
(6) _____	(f) Crew shifts weight to opposite side
	(g) Crew pays sheet out hand over hand

5. In Figure 59 below, show which boats are going from
   (a) a beat to a reach _____
   (b) a reach to a beat _____
   (c) a reach to a run _____
   (d) port tack to starboard tack _____

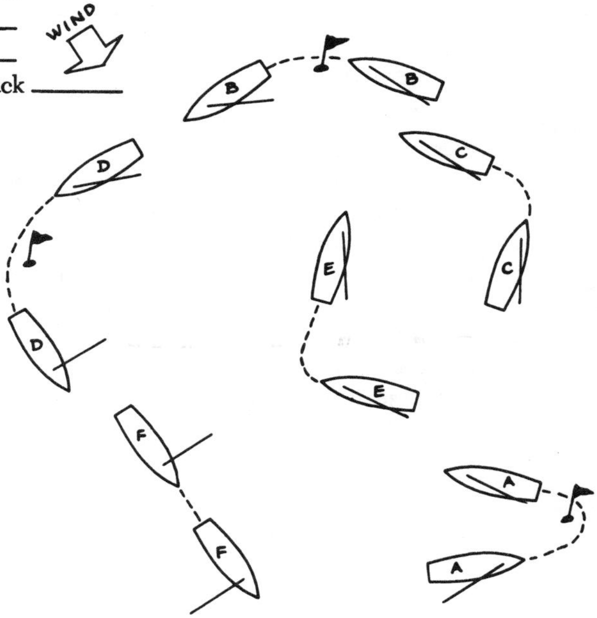

Fig. 59.

72

6. You have just changed course. What do you do if
    (a) the sail is already luffing?
    (b) the sail is not luffing?
    (c) you can't get the luff out, even after trimming sail in all the way?
7. What are the two most important factors in preventing an accidental jibe?
8. The wind is blowing your boat against the dock. What is a good way to shove off?
    If the wind is blowing your boat away from the dock, but there are boats on each side of you, what is a good way to shove off?
9. Name four steps you can take to make sure your boat won't be damaged by tying it up at a dock.
10. Answer true or false:
    (a) _____ The anchor line should be four times as long as the water is deep.
    (b) _____ Swinging anchor from side to side or overhead is recommended because you can aim it better.
    (c) _____ Standing on anchor line is just as good as making one end fast to the boat.
    (d) _____ The boat should be stopped or gathering some sternway before an anchor is heaved from the bow.
    (e) _____ Sometimes an anchor is lowered off the stern while the boat is still moving in to make a landing.
    (f) _____ Boat can approach mooring on a reach, if going slowly.
    (g) _____ The more anchor line you put out, the less chance the anchor has of holding.
    (h) _____ To pull the sheet in hand over hand means to roll it up on both hands as fast as possible.
    (i) _____ The side opposite the boat's boom is the name of the tack the boat is sailing on.

PRACTICE DRILL

1. Before going out, determine the direction of the wind and decide if it is too strong or not. (One way to tell is if there are other boats out.)
2. Set out a small flag on a wooden float, or use a mooring with plenty of clear water around it. Practice sailing up to this marker as if it were a mooring. Try to get so you can round up to this mark and stop just before you touch it, then gather sternway (being in irons), and get out of irons properly. This is a basic maneuver and one which you must be able to do well in order to sail at all.
3. Place three anchored objects in the water to form a large triangular course around which you can sail. You may use anchored boats or other buoys if they have plenty of water around them. The idea is to sail around the outside of these objects, tacking or jibing where necessary, and trimming sail

properly in between. *Make the course short.* Even a few hundred feet is good. Sailing out a half mile will not teach you how to maneuver or trim sails properly. Learn these fundamentals first. After sailing around your course many times, sail around in the opposite direction.

4. Practice jibing with crew. Sail on a run, and jibe your boat every two or three boat lengths. Then round up and beat back to the place you started, coming about every three or four boat lengths.

5. Try heaving a small anchor. Practice at first on the pier or on shore. Make the line fast to a post, coil it properly, and toss the anchor gently. Repeat until you can do it well.

5. Water Safety

1. The need for care. In no other sport is the price for carelessness so great as in sailing. The sea has claimed hundreds of lives because of ignorance, foolishness, or lack of common sense.

On the other hand, youngsters hardly big enough to hold a tiller can sail safely if they know the rules and obey them.

2. The swimming requirement. Every sailor, in fact everyone who takes to a boat, must be a swimmer. It is no good to say you won't be the one to tip over, because you may. The basic swimming requirement is to be able to swim at least ten boat lengths, and to be able to tread water indefinitely.

People who can't swim have an instinctive fear of the water. When they are in a boat this fear may turn to panic, especially if things get bad — a sudden wind squall, a wave crashing over the bow, or a broken mast. It is this panic which causes the tragedy, for cool heads can weather any storm.

If there is any doubt about your swimming ability, stay ashore until you've learned. If any poor swimmer is to go out in your boat, have him wear a life jacket.

Reef

3. How to keep from tipping over (capsizing). If your boat is heeling (tipping) too much, so there is danger of capsizing or taking water over the leeward side, it is because of one or two things. First, you may not have enough weight on the windward side of the boat to balance it. You and your crew may both have to sit on the windward rail (the side or gunwale to windward). Secondly, there may simply be too much wind pushing on your sail. In this case, letting the sail out will let some of the wind go by. This is called *spilling* wind from the sail.

This is another good reason to keep the sail trimmed at the point where it is just about to luff. Wind can be spilled quickly by letting the sail out a little way, rather than having to let it out a long distance.

Another method of spilling wind from the sail is to head the boat up into the wind until the sail luffs. The wind spills, and the boat stops heeling.

The experienced sailor combines both of these methods (Fig. 60) when the wind is strong, squalls hit, or the boat tips danger-

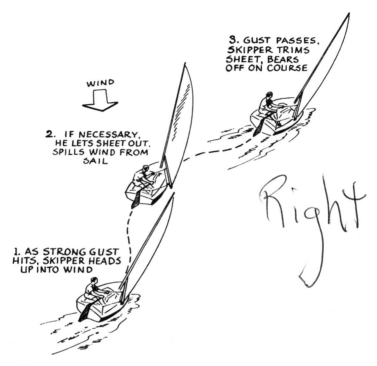

Fig. 60. The experienced skipper heads up into the wind and lets sail out when strong wind hits.

ously. However, be careful that you don't round up too far and get in irons. Try and keep some headway at all times so you can continue to steer.

If you are sailing on a broad reach or a run, it may be very diffi- *whoops* cult to head up or even spill the wind. Here the best thing to do is run before the storm, keeping your headway (and ability to steer), and hope to find some shelter behind an island, a point of land, or a dock. At least you can usually get close to shore, where there is less danger, and you can actually sail the boat right up on the beach if necessary!

HA !! maybe slowly round up

4. Don't tie the sheet down. When sailing, never secure your sheet to a cleat with half hitches (Fig. 61). They are hard to get off, and you won't be able to let the sail out rapidly. If the line gets wet and swollen, you may have to cut the sheet to let out sail.

NEVER MAKE SHEET FAST WITH HALF HITCH

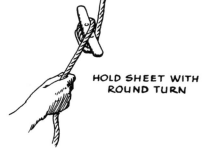

TO SAIL

Fig. 61. Hold sheet with a round turn on cleat, not a half hitch.

HOLD SHEET WITH ROUND TURN

If the wind is strong, it is all right to take a half turn or full turn around a cleat to help hold the sheet. But don't tie it down!

On larger yachts, if the tack is long and the wind steady, a slippery hitch may be used. However, it is not recommended for use on small boats (in the 8- to 16-foot group) or for beginners. It jams too often, especially when wet.

5. Stow all lines. Keep shipshape. This means keep your cockpit neat. Halyards should be coiled and stored forward (see Chapter 1). All loose gear should be stowed (put away) or tied in place. The mainsheet should be loose in the bottom and not tangled on fittings or the centerboard well.

Life jackets should be kept where they can be gotten easily if you capsize. Don't stow them way up under a deck or in a locker. Keep them near the middle of the cockpit.

6. No foolishness. There is no place for horseplay in the boat. The sea can be cruel, but sailing is a safe sport when the fun aboard is well salted with common sense. Don't take chances; be safe and sensible.

7. What to do if you tip over. Capsizing is an experience shared by nearly all who sail. It is not dangerous if you follow certain steps:

(1) Find your crew and make sure he is all right.

(2) Put on your life jacket. Do this regardless of whether you are an expert swimmer or not. The jacket adds warmth as well as safety and will help save your energy.

(3) Stay with the boat. Boats are *always* found after the storm, people are not. Even a small wooden rowboat can keep ten or twelve adults afloat when swamped!

(4) Find your paddle or other gear, but don't swim away from the boat for it. Sit or hang on your boat and wait for rescue. If at sea, tie yourself to your crew by a length of any available line.

8. Towing the swamped boat. When the rescue boat arrives, get the crew aboard and safe. Now you will want to tow in.

First untie halyards and sheets and remove sails. With the boat on its side, pull centerboard down, climb on it, and help right the boat. If the sea is not too rough, it is best at this point to bail out as much water as possible. You will have to bail fast, as some water will come back in the centerboard well. To slow this, stuff rope or cloth in the well around the centerboard so you can get more water out than comes in.

With the boat upright, secure a towline through your *bow chock* and around your mast. Do not use the deck cleat, as the boat full of water is too heavy a load and the cleat will pull loose.

If the boat cannot be righted, unstep the mast and remove it. Never tow the boat with mast or sails in the water, as the mast will break and the sails tear. Someone can sit in the stern of the towed boat and help to steer, but he should wear a life jacket.

9. Use of life jackets. Life jackets are necessary equipment on all boats. One jacket for every person aboard. So-called "life cushions" are not sufficient. They cannot be worn, and in most cases they will not support a person's weight in the water. Never go out in any boat without a life jacket for every person.

When bad weather threatens, or storm squalls are approaching, put on your life jacket. It is somewhat bulky, but warm and wind-proof. It is a lot easier to put it on while you are dry and sailing than when you are wet and in the water. Use only United States Coast Guard approved jackets. Kapok or foam-filled jackets are best.

10. Safe approach to the dock. As discussed in Chapter 1, always land on the leeward side of a dock (downwind side), so you can head directly into the wind with sail luffing.

If your boat is large enough to have a deck on the bow, crew should move forward and take a sitting position with feet out in front to act as bumper. In this way he can fend off with strong legs if you are coming in too fast. Standing on the bow allows no way to fend off. However, do not get a hand or foot caught between the dock and the gunwale of the boat.

On larger yachts, the pole or pike may be used. Hold it to your side, not in front, so you are not thrown off balance when taking up the strain of landing.

11. How to slow a boat down. In an emergency, boats under 12 or 15 feet may be slowed down at the landing by throwing the mainsail over and forcibly pushing it out against the wind. This acts like a brake or parachute, but will only work when the boat is heading into the wind. It should be done only in emergency to avoid collisions.

12. Avoiding collisions. Regardless of who has the right of way or who is wrong, avoid a collision at all cost. The expensive damage to boats and sails is not worth proving a small point. Only a poor sailor or bad sportsman would let an accident happen that could be prevented.

13. Artificial resuscitation. Sometimes called "artificial respiration," this is a means of helping someone breathe who cannot, usually a victim of electric shock or drowning.

In the event of a drowning, you must know some form of artificial resuscitation. Unless there is an expert standing right there, this lifesaving procedure will depend on you. The man on the spot has to do it.

The method of mouth-to-mouth breathing described here can be done by anyone. Even small Boy Scouts have revived adults weighing over 200 pounds using this method. It is the most effective way known and is now recommended by the American National Red Cross and leading medical groups.*

In using artificial resuscitation, the most important thing to remember is, START AT ONCE. Don't wait for approval or examination or a more comfortable place. Begin in the boat, on the dock, or on the shore. The main thing is, get started! Here is how easy it is to do.

14. Method of mouth-to-mouth resuscitation. (See Fig. 62.)†

(a) Clear the air passages. Turn the victim face down so any water can drain out rapidly. Turn his head to the side and clean out his mouth and throat with your fingers or a cloth.

Strike the victim sharply between the shoulder blades with the flat of your hand to dislodge any fluid or debris caught in the lower throat. This should all take only a few seconds. Start mouth-to-mouth breathing at once, but cleaning procedure may be repeated whenever necessary.

(b) Turn the victim on his back, and kneel close to his right ear. Tip his head back as far as it will go easily. Put your thumb (which may be wrapped for protection) in his mouth between the teeth, and grasp the jaw under the chin with your fingers.

(c) Now pull forcefully upward on the lower jaw, pulling toward the top of the head and straightening the neck. This position is very important, because it keeps the air passages open and prevents the tongue from blocking the throat.

(d) Pinch the victim's nose closed with your left hand.

(e) Take a deep breath, place your mouth firmly over the victim's mouth, and blow forcefully into his lungs. A light cloth or handkerchief may be placed over mouth for æsthetic reasons, if desired.

(f) Watch the victim's chest. When it rises, take your mouth off his mouth, and he will exhale without assistance. Repeat blowing into his mouth about twenty times each minute. Blow gently if the victim is a small child or infant. *every three seconds*

---

* A full report on the mouth-to-mouth resuscitation method is given by the National Academy of Sciences – National Research Council in the May 17, 1958, issue of *The Journal of the American Medical Association.*

† Reproduced on page 80 by permission of The American Red Cross, Washington, D.C.

(g) Treat for shock as soon as possible. While mouth-to-mouth breathing is proceeding, blankets and coats should be placed under and over the victim's body and his feet should be elevated slightly. When he is breathing on his own, the victim may be given mild stimulants, but should be kept lying down and well wrapped up until experienced evaluation is made.

Don't give up. Some people have been resuscitated for hours — when all hope should have been lost — only to have full recovery.

SUMMARY OF STEPS
IN MOUTH-TO-MOUTH BREATHING:

(1) START AT ONCE. Don't wait for someone else.
(2) Clean out the victim's mouth and throat.
(3) Strike the victim between the shoulder blades.
(4) Turn victim on back. Put thumb in his mouth and pull jaw and head up and back.
(5) Pinch victim's nose with other hand.
(6) Cover his mouth tightly with your mouth. Blow in forcefully, about twenty time each minute.
(7) Repeat cleaning of mouth whenever needed.
(8) Keep victim warm. Treat for shock.

A. Clean out mouth, then strike sharply on back to clear throat.

B. Pull jaw and head back.

C. Hold jaw with one hand, then pinch nose with other.

D. Cover mouth tightly, blow forcefully into lungs, then release.

Fig. 62.   Mouth-to-mouth resuscitation.

BASIC KNOTS AND SEAMANSHIP

Heaving a line or a life ring.

Use: Throwing a small mooring line to dock or another boat. Throwing line or life ring in an emergency.

A. *Heaving a line.*

Step 1: Start at fastened end of line. Coil line neatly, laying each loop next to last one, in left hand.

Step 2: Split coil into two even sections, one in each hand.

Step 3: Swing coil in right hand *vertically,* aiming toward your target.

Step 4: Let coil go at top of swing. Open fingers of left hand so other coils will run off.

B. *Throwing a life ring.* The same steps are followed, but life ring takes the place of first coil that is thrown. *Throw beyond victim.* Be sure ring lands behind victim so he can grab line or ring as it is pulled toward him.

EXERCISES

QUESTIONS

1. If you were choosing another person to be your crew, would you want him to be a swimmer or a non-swimmer? _____
   Why? _____
2. What three things can you do to keep boat from tipping over too far?
3. Why is it dangerous to use a locking half hitch in holding sheet to a cleat?
4. Where are the life jackets kept on any boat? _____
   Where do you keep your halyard? _____ Your sheet? _____
5. When you tip over, what is the first thing to do? _____
   Can you swim or duck under water with a life jacket on? _____
   If the sea is rough, is it better to stay with the boat or try to swim for shore as long as you have a life jacket on? _____
6. Rescue boat has arrived. What things should you do before getting towed in? _____
7. Multiple choice. Choose the one best answer:
   (a) If mouth-to-mouth breathing seems necessary, you (should wait until you can get victim on pier or shore; wait until a doctor says victim is not breathing; start at once, even if in the bottom of a boat).
   (b) In mouth-to-mouth breathing it is important to (put your thumb in victim's mouth, pull victim's jaw up and back, rub legs and arms to keep victim warm).
   (c) If you approach dock too fast, have crew (fend off with his hand,

fend off with his feet, leap off boat to get on dock where he can fend off better).

(d) Life jackets are (to be kept up under the forward deck, for sissies only, bulky but warm, not as good as life cushions).

8. Answer true or false:

(a) _____ Mouth-to-mouth breathing is only for experts.

(b) _____ If the victim's head is bent forward instead of backward, air may not go into his lungs at all.

(c) _____ In general, you are not likely to pick up any germs from mouth-to-mouth breathing of a drowning victim.

(d) _____ If you are tipped over only 20 feet from shore, it is all right to "swim for it."

(e) _____ A sailboat can be towed safely on its side with the mast on, provided the rescue boat has a powerful enough engine.

(f) _____ Running your fingers way back into the victim's mouth is not a good way to clean it out.

(g) _____ A 12-foot sailboat might hold up twelve people in the water if it is swamped.

PRACTICE DRILL

1. On your next rainy day, review Chapters 1, 2, 3, and 4. Take your model boats and fan, and try to show what happens when making all maneuvers: going from reach to run, reach to beat, beat to run, and run to beat.

2. Use models and fan to demonstrate how to keep boat from capsizing. Tie sheet down close-hauled. Bring fan next to sail until model tips over. Next time do the same thing, but head model toward fan. What happens? Then, try the same thing with sheet loosened. What happens now?

3. Check your boat to see if it has the required equipment for your class. Is there a life jacket for each person?

4. Trade in or give away any life cushions you have and replace with approved life jackets or vests.

5. Next time you sail, put on life jacket and try your basic maneuvers: jibing, coming about, etc. Notice how different it is to move about with jacket on, but that it adds warmth as well as protection.

6. If there is good swimming where you are, capsize a small rowboat or sailboat. Find as many friends as you can and see how many people the boat will hold up, all hanging on to one side or the other.

6. Elementary Sailboat Racing

1. What racing is all about. If you have ever seen sailboats bunched together on the water, heard the starting gun boom, and seen the boats sail off in what seemed like all different directions, you have probably wondered what sailboat racing is all about. It is really quite simple.

The object is to start together, sail around a course, and try to get back first. The racing course is an imaginary path on the water, usually marked by flags anchored at various places. It may also be marked by anchored boats, navigation buoys, or pilings (wooden posts) in the water. Whatever is used, they are called *course markers*. Boats must go around each one in a designated order (Fig. 63).

Fig. 63.   Some types of course markers used in racing.

Class races. Boats that are built alike, from the same plans, are *class boats.* Each class has a name, such as Moth, Sabot, Comet, Star, etc., and a set of regulations telling what size and shape the boats can be. Since larger boats with more sail can go faster, a class race with boats of the same size is fairer.

Regattas. Boats of two or three different classes may race over the same course together, but they start at different times — usually five minutes apart — and race against boats in their own class only. When boats sail a series of races over a one-, two-, three-day or longer period, the series is called a regatta. There may be one class of boats or many classes competing for one or more trophies, or prizes.

Handicap and cruising races. In larger yachts, 20 or 30 feet or more in length, there are many different designs, lengths, and sizes racing against each other. The boats with more sail — the slimmer boats, the boats with tall, narrow sails — go faster than the others. Each boat is given a *rating,* or *handicap,* depending on these factors and its size.

To give a *handicap* is to give a small runner a 10- or 15-foot head start over a bigger one. In ocean racing, boats sail over the same distance, but compare which does it in the least time. The handicap is made by adding so many minutes and hours to the faster boats, making their time for the course closer to that of the slower boats.

The *cruising races* go longer distances, have course markers for start and finish, but may sail around islands or lighthouses on the way. A day's cruise may start at Newport Beach, California, and sail around Santa Catalina Island and back . . . or a longer cruise may go from Newport News, Virginia, all the way to the Bermuda Islands in the mid-Atlantic.

2. Basic racing courses for small boats. The most popular course for racing is the *triangular course.* It consists of three course marks (Fig. 64), and boats may sail around in one direction or the other, as determined beforehand.

As you sail around the course, each mark will be passed on the same side of your boat. When you pass each mark on your left, or port side, this is called *taking the marks to port.* When you *take the marks to starboard,* you pass them all on your starboard side.

If you towed an imaginary string around the race course, you could pull it tight at the finish, and all the marks of the course would be inside. If not, you went around one the wrong way!

Starting and finishing lines are set up by the race committee, who are the officials of the race and who generally have a small power boat with a race committee flag on it. On our diagrams we will represent them by a square flag with *RC* on it. Course markers are triangular flags (Fig. 64).

The start may be at any corner of the triangle. It is most often at a downwind, or leeward, mark, so that boats will start on a beat, working up into the wind. This is the best start, because boats getting to the line first get the better wind. If the start is downwind, on a run, the late boats that are behind in getting to the line will blanket and cut off the wind of those ahead. This is hardly fair, so a *windward start* is preferred.

The imaginary line between the first mark of the course and the committee boat flag is the *starting line*. It is set at right angles to the first leg of the course, and usually at right angles to the wind direction (Fig. 64).

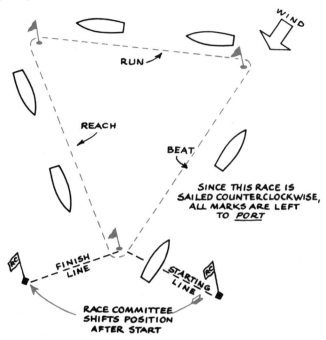

RUN

REACH

BEAT

WIND

SINCE THIS RACE IS SAILED COUNTERCLOCKWISE, ALL MARKS ARE LEFT TO *PORT*

FINISH LINE

STARTING LINE

RACE COMMITTEE SHIFTS POSITION AFTER START

Fig. 64. Triangular course showing a race in progress and how race committee may set start and finish line.

While the boats are out racing, the race committee generally moves its flag around so the finish line is at right angles to the last leg of the course, thus making it fairer for boats which are close together near the end of the race.

The second most popular racing course is the *windward-leeward course* (Fig. 65). Whereas the triangular course has three legs (a reach, a beat, and a run), the windward-leeward has but two (a beat and a run). The start may be at the leeward mark, or it may be half-way up the first leg.

Again you pass all marks to the same side, and if a string were towed in your wake it would gather up all the course markers inside it when you were finished. No part of the mark above water, including the flag, may be touched; otherwise you are disqualified. However, if you touch a part below water it is all right.

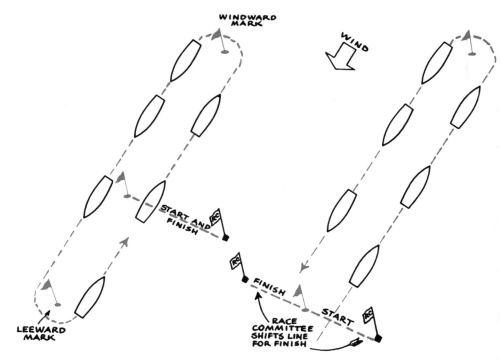

Fig. 65. Windward-leeward course
showing two starting lines.

3. How you start your race. By definition a boat starts at the instant any part of her hull or gear crosses the starting line.

The idea in starting is to be sailing across the line in the direction of the next mark at the time the starting gun fires. But how do you know when the gun will fire? The race committee helps you here by giving some warning signals beforehand (either flags or guns or both). These signals are given at exact times before the starting signal, so all you have to do is time them on your watch, and you will know when to start.

Starting signals. Most race committees use three signals for starts: *warning, preparatory,* and *start signals.* The warning signal is given ten minutes before the start, the preparatory signal is given five minutes before the start, and the start signal is given precisely at the start.

There are usually two signals given simultaneously: a *visual signal* — a hoisted flag, cylinder, cone, or other object (Fig. 66) — and a *sound signal* — a gun or whistle. Here is how they are used.

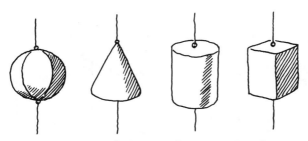

Fig. 66.   Objects used as start signals.

When it is exactly ten minutes before the start, a white flag is hoisted on the committee boat and a gun fired. This is the warning signal (Fig. 67).

The flag stays up exactly four and a half minutes, then is brought down half a minute before the next signal. This gives you warning that a new signal is coming in thirty seconds.

Five minutes before the start a blue flag is hoisted and a gun fired. This is the preparatory signal. This flag also stays up four and a half minutes and is brought down thirty seconds before the start.

At the start another gun is fired and a red flag is hoisted. This flag stays up and means that the race has begun.

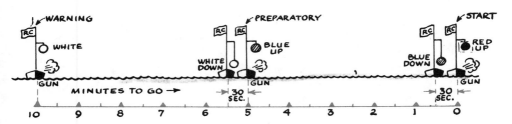

Fig. 67.   The "time to go" before the start is given by a visual signal and a gun.

The official start. Because a gun sometimes fails to go off, the race officially begins when the starting signal is hoisted. Sometimes objects other than flags are used. These are made of canvas and have a characteristic shape such as a ball, cylinder, or cone, so they can be easily recognized at a greater distance than flags.

Use of a stop watch. Most sailors use a stop watch for racing, but any waterproof watch with a sweep second hand is good enough.

A stop watch for sailors shows the time remaining before the start in minutes and seconds. A quick push on the watch stem starts it at ten minutes to go, and the time remaining can be read directly from the dial.

SUMMARY OF STARTING SIGNALS:

Time Before Start	Signal	Color and Position	Sound
10 min.	warning	white, up	gun
5½ min.		white, down	
5 min.	preparatory	blue, up	gun
½ min.		blue, down	
0 min.	start	red, up	gun

Some yacht clubs and fleets may use a shortened time schedule for starting signals, especially if the boats are under 12 or 14 feet in length and do not need much time to get ready for their starts.

This may be done by having the warning signal hoisted five minutes before the start and the preparatory signal hoisted one minute before the start. Colors are the same, guns or whistle sounds are used, and each signal is lowered half a minute before the next signal is due.

4. How a typical race begins. The race committee will tell you what the course is and where the marks are. They may do this ashore, or they may post it by big numbers on a sign on their boat.

You will have a racing circular which will tell you the starting signals. It may read as follows:

1. Warning signal. Ten minutes before start.
   Hoisting of white cylinder. Gun.
2. Preparatory signal. Five minutes before start.
   Hoisting of blue cone. Gun.
3. Start. Hoisting of red cube. Gun.

Before the start you may sail across the starting line as often as you wish to for practice. As the signals are given, you or your crew start the watch and keep track of the time. At the start signal you try to be crossing the line heading for the next mark.

You may sail around the course once, twice, or even three times, as announced by the race committee, then cross the finish line.

All through the race you are sailing close to other boats, crossing their paths — or they are crossing yours. In each instance there is a rule which tells you who has the right of way. In order to race, you have to learn the rules.

5. The basic rules in racing. There are nearly seventy different rules governing sailboat racing, and many parts to each of these. They were set up by the governing body of the sport, the North American Yacht Racing Union.

Of these rules and definitions, we will discuss only those which have to do with right of way. These tell you whether you have to get out of the way of another boat or whether she has to get out of your way. These rules are just as important as knowing which side of the road you drive a car on, or what you do at a stop light, or who has right of way at an intersection.

In racing when a rule is not followed it is a *foul*, and the boat is disqualified and has to drop out of the race. There does not have to be a collision of boats. Sailors speak of this as "fouling out." It is another good reason to know the rules.

We will start with four basic rules now, which will let you get started racing. These are important ones because they are used most often. The others will be discussed in later chapters.

Starboard TACK has Right of Way

(1) Opposite tack rule: When two boats are on opposite tacks, the port tack boat shall keep clear.

This means that when you are sailing on a port tack (wind coming over port side) and there is a boat approaching on the starboard tack (Fig. 68), you must get out of her way. This is called *keeping clear*.

You can keep clear by tacking before she reaches you or by falling off and passing behind her. With practice you will know which one to do in any condition.

When beating to windward on a port tack, you and your crew must constantly look under your sail for starboard tack boats and be sure you give them right of way.

When running free or on a reach the rule also applies, and it makes no difference if the other boat is running or reaching, so long as it is on the opposite tack. In each case, starboard tack boat has right of way, and port tack boat keeps clear.

Whenever you are approaching a second boat, the first thing to consider is: What tack is she on? Then: What tack am I on?

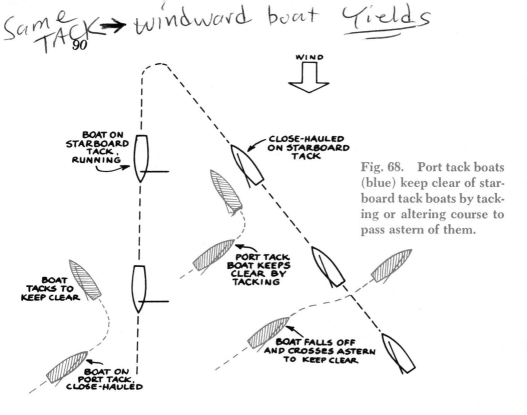

Fig. 68.   Port tack boats (blue) keep clear of starboard tack boats by tacking or altering course to pass astern of them.

Suppose you look and find that you and the other boat are on the same tack, either both on port or both on starboard tack. Here the *same tack rule* applies. The rule has two parts:

(2) Same tack rule: (a) If two boats are on the same tack, the windward boat keeps clear (Fig. 69).

How much clear?

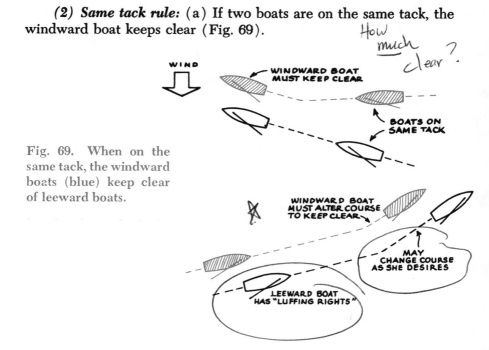

Fig. 69.   When on the same tack, the windward boats (blue) keep clear of leeward boats.

Here is when this rule applies. First, the boats must be within two boat lengths of each other. Secondly, they must be on the same tack and must *overlap*. If a line drawn across the bow of one boat will cross the other (Fig. 70), then they overlap. The side of each boat that the boom is over is the leeward side, the other is the wind-

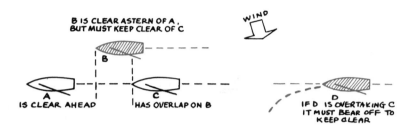

Fig. 70. When a line drawn across the bow of one boat will cross another, they *overlap*. Otherwise the rear boat (blue) is *clear astern* and must keep clear.

ward side. One boat is to windward of the other, and this one must keep clear.

This rule applies whether you are beating, reaching, or on a run, provided you are both on same tack (Fig. 72).

Luffing rights. Since the boat to windward must keep clear, the leeward boat can alter course to windward and force the other boat to do the same, even until sails are luffing and boats are heading dead into the wind. The leeward boat calls this her "luffing rights."

If you do not overlap, then one boat is *clear astern* and the other is *clear ahead.* The boat that is behind was once called the *overtaking boat,* a term no longer used. Nevertheless she is obliged to keep clear of boats ahead. Here the second part of the rule applies.

(2) Same tack rule: (b) If two boats are on the same tack, the boat clear astern shall keep clear of the boat clear ahead (Fig. 70).

This means that if you are catching up with the boat ahead and she is on the same tack, you must keep out of her way. If she is on the other tack, then the opposite tack rule applies.

Establishing an overlap. An overlap is established whenever the bow or any part of the overtaking boat has caught up with any part of the other boat (Fig. 71). If you overlap on the leeward side, you have right of way since the windward boat must keep clear.

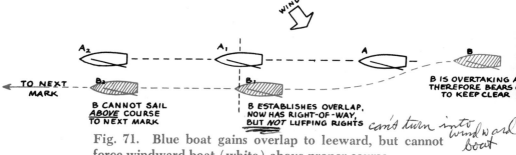

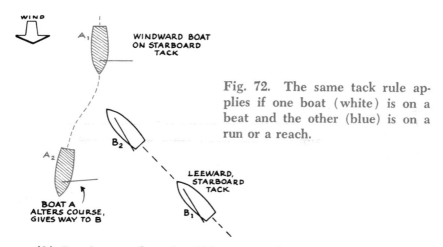

Fig. 71. Blue boat gains overlap to leeward, but cannot force windward boat (white) above proper course.

When running free or on a reach. When you are on a run, be sure you keep an eye out for boats approaching you on a beat (Fig. 72). If they are on the same tack, then you must keep clear, since you are windward boat.

Fig. 72. The same tack rule applies if one boat (white) is on a beat and the other (blue) is on a run or a reach.

(3) Passing marks rule: If boats overlap on reaching a mark, the outside boat must give the inside boat room to pass or round her (Fig. 73).

This means that as you are coming to a mark, there may be boats inside you next to the mark and others outside you away from the mark (Fig. 73). If the inside boats overlap you before you start to

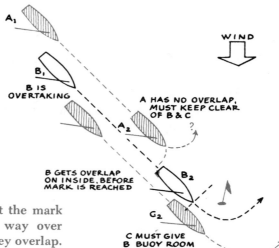

WIND

A₁

B₁

B IS
OVERTAKING

A HAS NO OVERLAP,
MUST KEEP CLEAR
OF B & C

A₂

B GETS OVERLAP
ON INSIDE, BEFORE
MARK IS REACHED

B₂

C₂

C MUST GIVE
B BUOY ROOM

Fig. 73. Boats inside at the mark (white) have right of way over other boats outside, if they overlap.

overlap

turn, then you must give them enough space to round the mark without hitting it. Sailors refer to this as "buoy room."

If you have established an overlap on the boats outside you at the mark, they will give you buoy room. If you have no overlap, then you are simply the overtaking boat and must keep clear of them. Does it make any difference if you are on the same or opposite tacks? Yes and no. Here is why.

At the leeward mark. It makes no difference whether you are on port or starboard tack when rounding the leeward mark (the one farthest downwind). The passing marks rule applies even if it is a port tack boat claiming buoy room from a starboard tack boat (Fig. 74).

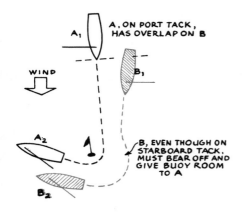

A₁

A, ON PORT TACK,
HAS OVERLAP ON B

B₁

WIND

A₂

B, EVEN THOUGH ON
STARBOARD TACK,
MUST BEAR OFF AND
GIVE BUOY ROOM
TO A

B₂

Fig. 74. At the leeward mark, boats may be on opposite *or* same tack to claim "buoy room."

At the windward mark. When beating to windward and approaching the weather mark (the one farthest upwind), the opposite tack rule applies first (Fig. 75). Before claiming an overlap or room at the mark, boats must be on the same tack.

This is a common-sense ruling, since the windward mark can be rounded only on one tack and boats approaching on the other tack would have to come about at the mark, causing a great deal of confusion.

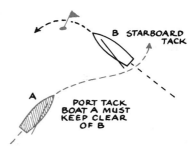

Fig. 75. At the windward mark, the opposite tack rule comes first.

(4) Tacking and jibing rule: When a boat tacks or jibes, she must keep clear of other boats sailing on a tack.

This rule means that you cannot tack or jibe directly in front of another boat, or in such a way that she has to change course to avoid hitting you (Fig. 76).

If your tack or jibe will put you into a position so you will have right of way that you did not have over a boat before, you must allow the other boat time to maneuver out of your way. And the other boat does not have to give you right of way until your tack or jibe is completed.

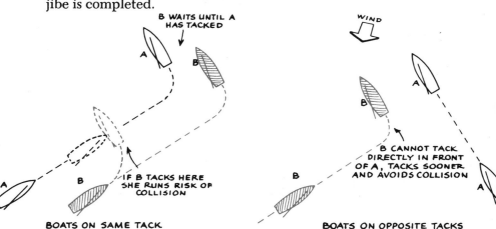

Fig. 76. A boat cannot tack or jibe if other boats are so close they will collide before the tack is completed.

SUMMARY OF FOUR BASIC RULES:
(1) Opposite tack rule: Port tack keeps clear.
(2) Same tack rule: (a) Windward boat keeps clear;
    (b) Boat clear astern keeps clear of boat ahead.
(3) Passing marks rule: Overlapping boat has right to
    buoy room.
(4) Tacking and jibing rule: Boat tacking or jibing must
    keep clear.

6. Examples of racing rules in use. When you are out sailing it is impossible to get out the rule book and check on who has the right of way. Here are situations which come up in most races. Study these and see how the four basic rules apply. You should know who has the right of way and who keeps clear in each case (Fig. 77). Rules at the start will be covered in Chapter 9.

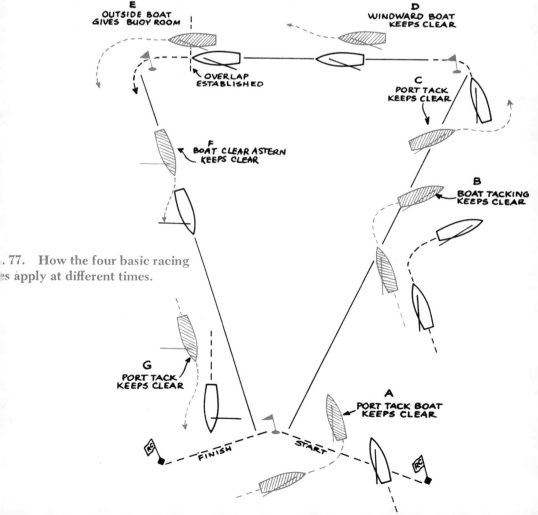

77. How the four basic racing
s apply at different times.

BASIC KNOTS AND SEAMANSHIP

Whipping a line. (Fig. 78)

Use: At the ends of line to keep it from fraying and unraveling. Temporarily, friction tape or adhesive tape may be wrapped around end of line . . . but the mark of a good sailor is a neat whipping of sailmaker's thread or marlin. However, any stout thread waxed with a candle or beeswax will do for most small lines.

> Step 1: Pass a few turns of twine around rope, then lay on a small loop of twine, pointing toward the end. Begin winding twine over itself.
> Step 2: Wind tightly and neatly, making whipping as long as rope is thick.
> Step 3: Place the end through part of loop sticking out.
> Step 4: Pull loop so end is buried in middle of splice. Cut off twine. Trim end of rope about half an inch from whipping.

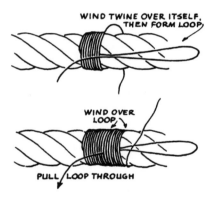

Fig. 78. Whipping.

Synthetic lines. Apply heat of match to end of synthetic line such as nylon, and end will melt and fuse threads together.

EXERCISES

1. Write short definitions for the following:
    (a) Course markers
    (b) Class boats
    (c) Triangular racing course
    (d) Windward-leeward course
    (e) Starting line
    (f) Opposite tacks
    (g) Same tacks
2. Multiple choice. Choose the one best answer:
    (a) In a race, the course marker goes by your boat on the right side. This is called (taking the mark to port, righting the mark, taking the mark to starboard).
    (b) The flag in the water at the opposite end of the starting line from the race committee is on your port side when you start your race. All other course markers will be passed on your (starboard side, port side, port side and then starboard side).
    (c) Your boat starts the race as soon as any part of the (mast, bow, stern, sail) crosses the starting line.
    (d) If both gun and flags are used, the race officially starts (at the sound of the gun, at the sight of the gun's flash and smoke, when the red flag is hoisted).
    (e) If there are five minutes between preparatory and start signals, the flag will stay up (two and a half, four and a half, five) minutes.
    (f) How many times should you sail around a triangular course? (Always just once, always just twice, the race committee will tell you.)
3. Why is a stop watch used in racing?
4. Write out the following four basic racing rules:
    (a) Opposite tack rule
    (b) Same tack rule
    (c) Passing marks rule
    (d) Tacking and jibing rule
5. Answer true or false:
    (a) _____ If a racing rule is not obeyed, but the boats do not hit, the offending boat may stay in the race.
    (b) _____ If you are half a boat length in front of another boat, you can probably tack safely and keep clear of her.
    (c) _____ When beating to the windward mark, the opposite tack rule applies before the passing marks rule.
    (d) _____ A boat running free always has right of way over a boat close-hauled.

(e) _____ The boat clear astern must keep clear while on the same tack. Otherwise, the opposite tack rule applies.

(f) _____ If two boats on the same tack do not overlap, then one must be clear ahead and the other clear astern if they are within two boat lengths of each other.

(g) _____ The racing rules do not apply if sailboats are of greatly different size.

6. On the diagram below (Fig. 79), black in each boat which must give right of way to the others that are near her. Write in the rule which applies.

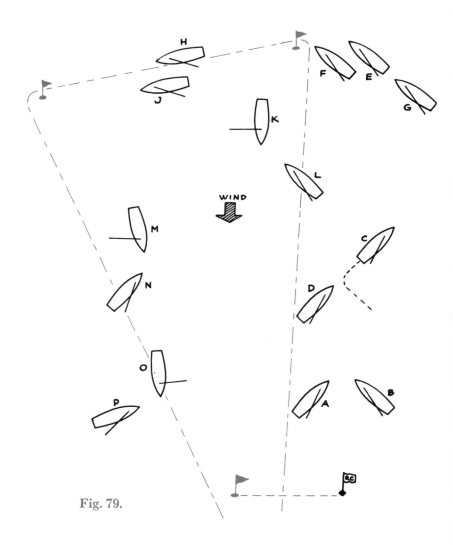

Fig. 79.

PRACTICE DRILL

1. Before you do any racing, set up your model boats in various situations. Have your crew tell you who has right of way, and why. Then have him test you. If alone, set them up in the positions shown in Figure 79. Memorize what each situation is and what rule applies.

2. Sail on a reach or beat with another boat of your class or size. Notice your speed compared to hers. Now trim your sheet so sail is pulled in far beyond the point of luffing. Notice how this slows boat. Now sail with a big luff in sail, then a very small luff, and notice how your speed changes.

3. Put out a single marker, or use a buoy with plenty of clear water around it. Sail to the marker and tack at once around it. Sail back, and approach it on a run and jibe around it. Next, sail toward it on a reach, then turn sharply around it by trimming in and coming to a beat, then come about. Repeat this drill over and over until you and the crew are experts at rounding marks. Now you are ready to race.

4. Try to sail in any race that you can. If in a club 'or sailing class, sail with your group over very short courses. These will give you more practice more often, both in rounding marks and in using the right-of-way rules. If you are just a guest in another fleet, you will have to sail whatever race they set. Try it anyway.

5. On each leg of your race, constantly trim your sails to get the most speed out of your boat for that particular heading. This is the way the champions race — working every minute — no matter how far behind.

6. Concentrate on the fundamentals. Don't worry about tactics or strategy of racing. Learn the basic rules. Learn how to trim your sail for the maximum speed on every leg. Learn how to come about smoothly and efficiently. These are the important things in racing now . . . the tactics will come later.

7. Sailing in Heavy Weather

1. How dangerous are strong winds? For the sailor who knows what he is doing, strong winds are not only safe, but they provide some of the greatest thrills in sailing.

Here are some safety precautions you should know and some tricks to help you before you sail in strong or "heavy" weather.

Limitations of your boat. You must know first how much punishment your boat can take. This depends on her age and condition. Is she strong enough to withstand the force of wind on mast and rigging? Is she large enough to ride over the waves which build up in strong winds? Are the sheets fairly new and not worn? Have the halyards been turned, so there is fairly new line in the top two or three feet? Running rigging and standing rigging must be checked and repaired thoroughly before you sail in strong winds.

If you don't know the limitations of your boat, watch and see what other people do. Natives of the area get to know the wind and weather pretty well and what size boat is safe. If they aren't going out, it is best for you not to, either.

Strong, steady winds vs. strong, puffy winds. When wind is steady, sailing is safer than when wind is puffy. It is the changeable wind — which is strong one minute, then light the next, or from one direction now and another in a few minutes — that is dangerous. Strong and puffy winds with many squalls (small storms) generally mean the weather is turning bad, and the wise sailor will wait it out.

If you do go out, remember to stay near shore. The wind is steadier, the waves are less, and it is safer should you tip over.

When is the wind too strong? This depends on the size of your boat. When whitecaps (white crests on the wave tops) first begin to appear, the wind is blowing about 11 to 16 knots (13 to 18 miles per hour). This is called a moderate breeze, and sailing is difficult in boats under 10 or 12 feet in length.

When the waves are long and whitecaps cover the water, it is called a fresh breeze. Wind is blowing at 17 to 21 knots (19 to 23 miles per hour), but may be considerably stronger in gusts. For boats of 16 to 20 feet this wind is safe, but the sailing is rough and wet.

A good general rule for beginners in small boats is to come in when whitecaps are covering the water.

Small craft warnings. The United States Coast Guard station in your area will fly a large red triangular flag when it is not safe for small boats to go out on the lake or ocean. Local weather reports in the newspaper usually predict wind changes and force with accuracy.

2. Keeping dry and warm. Sailing in strong winds inevitably means getting wet from sea spray and waves. Take along proper personal gear: waterproof jacket with hood or tight collar, waterproof pants or bathing suit, heavy sweater or two, gloves with fingers cut off to help you hold sheets, and even an extra pair of heavy socks for cold feet!

If you are caught without a waterproof jacket, put on all the shirts and sweaters you have. If they get soaking wet they will still add warmth, since your body will heat the wet inner layers and the outer layers will protect you from the wind. Don't forget your life jacket. Wear it. Its bulk adds warmth as well as safety.

3. Set and trim of sail. When the wind is strong, the sail needs less curve or belly. Otherwise the sail tends to luff sooner and in general will move the boat more slowly. Consequently, what you need to do is make your sail flatter.

This is done by pulling it out tight at all corners and edges. Set your outhaul and downhaul as tight as you can without making too many wrinkles in the sail. If your boat has a jibstay and head-stay you can put a little bow in the mast by tightening the lower stay and loosening the upper. The bow has the effect of flattening the middle section of the sail.

Leach line. This is a small line sometimes sewn in the hem of the leach and used to produce a deep pocket or "baggy" shape to the sail. It must be loosened in heavy weather.

Shaping sail with mainsheet. When the sail is trimmed close-hauled or nearly so, the sail can be flattened by moving the sheet block (pulley) on the deck or traveler more to the outside (Fig. 80). Since the boom is just about over the outer edge, this gives a more downward pull on the sail and tends to flatten it.

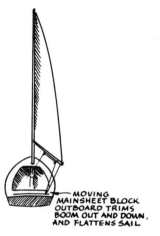

Fig. 80. The block for the main-sheet is moved outboard to flatten sail for heavy weather.

MOVING MAINSHEET BLOCK OUTBOARD TRIMS BOOM OUT AND DOWN, AND FLATTENS SAIL

Old sails. If you have a choice of more than one suit of sails, use old sails, particularly ones that are "blown out," or flattened from use, for sailing in heavy weather. Newer sails with deeper pockets are better in light breezes.

4. Securing sheets and halyards. Sheets are never cleated in heavy weather, as you have to be able to let them out immediately to spill wind if a puff hits. They are coiled loosely in the cockpit and kept free from tangling. Halyards are secured on cleats with round turns and crossing turns, but not locking half hitches (see Chapter 1). These are too hard to get out if wet or if the halyard must be let go in a hurry. Halyards are coiled neatly so they can be lowered quickly.

5. Trim of boat. Strong winds tend to make your boat heel considerably. It may be more thrilling to sail tipped way over like this, but you will actually sail faster *on an even keel* (boat more level).

This is true for at least two reasons. As the boat heels, wind spills over the top of the sail so there is less driving force working for you. Secondly, if your boat sails more upright, she rides on the flat portion of the hull and tends to skim over the water. This is faster than if she heels and buries the leeward chine deep in the waves.

Hiking straps. Many skippers fasten canvas straps or ropes inside their cockpits, running crossways, to hook their feet under (Fig. 81). These are called hiking straps and let you hang out over the gunwales (hike out) to help balance the boat. They are used when racing to windward, and should have hooks or snaps so you can take them off when sailing downwind.

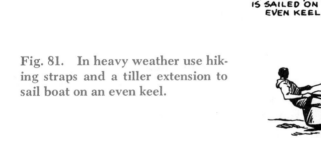

BY HIKING OUT AND USING TILLER EXTENSION, BOAT IS SAILED ON AN EVEN KEEL

Fig. 81.   In heavy weather use hiking straps and a tiller extension to sail boat on an even keel.

Tiller extension. A second racing device to help you sit as far outboard as possible is the tiller extension. It is a small wooden arm which is hinged to the end of your tiller (Fig. 81) and lets you lean way back without pulling the tiller with you. A wooden extension with finger grips is better than a rope extension because you will have to push on the tiller as well as pull on it.

Where to sit. In general, you and your crew should sit together near the centerboard well, which is just at the pivot point of your boat. This will let the boat come about more easily. Depending on the wind, you will shift your weight outboard (out on the gunwale, or hiking) or inboard (toward the inside) to sail boat on an even keel.

When beating to windward your boat will tend to round up into the wind if you let go of the tiller. This is called a *weather helm.* It will let you spill wind or luff sail much more quickly. If you let go the tiller and the boat falls off, this is called a *lee helm,* and is undesirable.

In very strong winds boats usually have a great deal of weather helm. Some weather helm is all right, but too much slows you down. To reduce weather helm, move yourself and crew aft a foot or two. Further discussion of weather helm will be found in Chapter 11.

6. Keeping boat dry. In heavy weather spray will blow over your bow. Waves will come in over the bow and over the lee rail. Sometimes waves will come over the stern!

Fighting water becomes a big problem. To keep water out, use spray rails on deck. They should be wide enough to deflect water away from the cockpit.

Use a bailing scoop or can, and have an extra one aboard. Many a bailer has been thrown overboard accidentally by an eager sailor. Keep a second one aboard and tie it in.

A small pump that can be worked by foot is good for large amounts of water. These, and larger hand pumps, may have small metal "feet" that should be covered with tape; otherwise the metal edges chew up the wood in your bilge.

In a race the best time to bail is when sailing on a reach or on the downwind leg, when crew is not so busy just helping to balance boat.

7. Weather signs and what to look for. To be a good sailor you must know about weather, for two reasons: first for your own safety, and second to provide you with information that will help you win races. You must acquire an ability not only to tell when the weather is turning bad, but also to tell when and where new wind will be coming.

Thunderstorms. For small-boat sailors who go out for a day or an afternoon of sailing, the main weather problem is the thunderstorm. These can be dangerous and must be taken seriously. They are common during the summer, and occur late in the day after the heat of the sun.

The storm begins with a darkening sky and the appearance of a typical "thunderhead." This is a massive vertical cloud formation, called *cumulo-nimbus*, which has "a dirty bottom and an anvil top," with whitecaps and rain underneath (Fig. 82).

Fig. 82. Cumulo-nimbus clouds.

STRONG DOWNDRAFTS

← DANGER AREA →

SUDDEN STRONG, SHIFTING WINDS
ACCOMPANIED BY SHARP
TEMPERATURE DROP

The storms are of short duration and so do not build up waves of any great extent. Your chief concern will be the wind. From the time you see the thunderhead, you have only about a half hour before the wind strikes. You have to make shore at once, or else take down your sail and ride out the storm (see Section 9, below).

You can't tell when and where the wind will hit. Moderate winds may blow first toward the storm; then sudden cold gusts may strike savagely in the other direction, capsizing your boat. After the wind, the temperature drops. Then comes the rain.

Use local weather reports. It is wise to get in the habit of checking the daily weather news on the radio or in the paper, especially if you are going out for a whole day or longer. These are United States Weather Bureau reports and will give you good predictions.

The falling barometer. The barometer is an instrument for measuring the pressure of the atmosphere. It used to be a tube of mercury about 30 inches in height and sealed at the top. Pressure changes caused it to "rise" and "fall." Most barometers today are the aneroid type, which contain no mercury. The dial is read in inches and decimals. An average pressure reading on a summer day in the United States might be 30.00 inches. Depending on the place, 29.50 inches might be low, and 30.50 inches high.

A falling barometer may mean wet weather, stronger winds, or southerly winds (from the south, southeast or southwest). If the temperature is rising at the same time, expect heavy rain.

If the barometer falls slowly for several days with fine weather, expect considerable rain.

If the weather stays clear and the barometer continues to be low, expect a sudden change in the weather or rain within twenty-four hours. A rising barometer means just the opposite, fair weather.

Sailors refer to the barometer as "the glass," and say this ditty:

> *When the glass falls low*
> *Prepare for a blow.*
> *When it rises high*
> *Let all your sails fly.*

Cloud formations. There are three types of cloud formations you should know. The thunderhead, or *cumulo-nimbus*, we have discussed. It may come on us suddenly and show only as a dark line of clouds across the horizon, with its huge anvil top being too high and far away to see.

Cumulus clouds are the fair-weather clouds. Seen on a bright summer day, they have rounded edges, appear bright and fleecy, and have rather flat bottoms. They mean good weather (Fig. 83).

CUMULUS
(FAIR-WEATHER CLOUDS)

CIRRUS
(CHANGING-WEATHER CLOUDS)

Fig 83.   Cumulus and cirrus clouds.

The third group is the *cirrus* family of clouds. They are high-flying and wispy. Sometimes they will bunch together to form fish scales, a so-called "mackerel sky." This group indicates the weather is changing, usually for the worse, but sometimes for the better (Fig. 83).

A glowing sunset at twilight is a fair-weather sign, but it is not true in the morning. Remember the wisdom in this sailors' jingle:

A red sky at night,
Is the sailor's delight.
A red sky in the morning,
Makes the sailor take warning.

If it is raining when you awaken, perhaps this rhyme will cheer you up:

Rain before seven
Clear by eleven.

8. Shortening sail. This means reducing the amount of sail that you have hoisted. When heavy weather hits, large yachts with many sails will take in one or more and sail on reduced canvas. In small boats you can either reef sail or use a storm sail.

Storm sails. This type of sail is made of heavier cloth than your everyday *working sail* (the one you use most often), and its size is smaller. By reducing size you reduce the force of the wind on the sail and boat, and sailing in the storm is easier.

Reefing sail. (Fig. 84). Most smaller vessels do not have storm sails, so to reduce their sail areas they *reef*. This means lowering the sail one, two, or more feet and retying it at the foot, along the boom, thus taking the lower sail area out of use. There are two methods of reefing.

Roller reefing. Some boats have a boom that can roll like a window shade and wind the sail up on them. Reefing is done by luffing up into the wind and lowering the sail while you or your crew roll it up on the boom. Take care to pull the sail out toward the clew while rolling in the reef, smoothing out wrinkles and preventing the sail from bunching or folding.

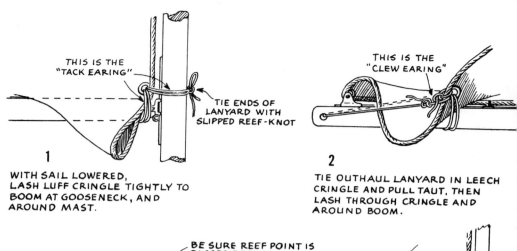

1

WITH SAIL LOWERED,
LASH LUFF CRINGLE TIGHTLY TO
BOOM AT GOOSENECK, AND
AROUND MAST.

2

TIE OUTHAUL LANYARD IN LEECH
CRINGLE AND PULL TAUT, THEN
LASH THROUGH CRINGLE AND
AROUND BOOM.

3

STARTING AT MIDDLE, AND WORKING BOTH WAYS,
FURL SAIL SNUGLY, AND TIE REEF POINTS, USING
SLIPPED REEF-KNOT.

Fig. 84.   Steps in reefing sail.

How to reef a sail with reef points. Don't underestimate the wind. If there are whitecaps, you will need a reef. And it is easier to put in a reef while on shore than when out in a strong blow. Here is how to do it (Fig. 84).

Reef points are small cords sewn into grommets (small brass rings) on the sail. At each end of the line of reef points is a larger ring, called a cringle. The forward one is the *luff cringle,* the after one the *leech cringle.*

Experienced sailors reef by lowering the sail until the reef points are even with the boom. Beginners should lower the sail all the way, especially if out at sea, to avoid costly mistakes. Follow these steps:

(1) Lower sail entirely, or to the first set of reef points.
(2) Start with the luff cringle. Tie it to the boom at the gooseneck, then tie it around the mast.
(3) Tie an outhaul in the leech cringle. Stretch tight. Secure at the end of the boom.

(4) Tie the leech cringle around the boom. This is the *reef earing*. Take a few extra turns around the sail at the end.

(5) Pull out the rest of the sail and furl it snugly. This is the *bunt* of the sail.

(6) Start at the luff, and tie reef points around the sail. Use a square knot or a square knot with the end not pulled through. Do *not* tie under the boom.

(7) If you have grommets without reef points, start at the tack and pass a lacing line around the sail. Tie at the clew. Do *not* go under the boom.

Shaking out a reef. When the wind lets up you may want to take the reef out. Do it by lowering sail first. As you gain experience, you can shake it out while underway by untying the middle reef point and working toward both ends. Next let off the line at the luff cringle, then the outhaul, and finally the leech earing. Before you hoist sail, make certain all lines are cast off the boom.

9. What to do if caught in a storm at sea. If a storm catches you by surprise when you are on open water and too far from shore to get protection, you may have to ride it out.

Sails should be gotten down at the first sign of the approaching storm — the whitecaps or the rapidly darkening sky. Tie the sails securely around the boom, or take them off and stow up under your deck.

Next, keep the boat headed into the approaching wind and waves. If the boat turns crossways to the wind, the waves will roll it over or swamp you. To keep the bow into the wind and waves you will need a sea anchor, or drogue.

The *sea anchor* is anything that can be dragged to slow the boat down. By attaching it to the bow (or sometimes the stern) you can keep boat headed into the wind.

A canvas sea anchor is made like a funnel, with a second line attached to it to spill the water out when you bring it in. A makeshift sea anchor can be made from a pail, or planks lashed together, or simply long pieces of old rope or chain. Even a sail bag or bundled-up sail might do.

10. Technique of beating in strong wind. When the wind is getting stronger or changing direction, it often comes first in strong puffs. If these puffs are coming from a new direction, you can expect a major wind shift to this direction.

Sailing to windward in strong and puffy winds is exciting, especially in a race when you want to get up to windward as much as possible to beat other boats to the mark. Here is how to let the wind help you.

When a puff hits your sail, let your boat ease up into the wind. It will temporarily point higher than normal because of the increased force of the puff. As the puff lets up, fall off a bit to your previous course.

If you find the puffs are coming from ahead and causing you to luff and fall off, come about and sail on the other tack. Now the puffs will work for you and help you move up to windward.

Coming about. When the wind is strong and the seas are heavy, it is best to come about as little as possible. Every time you do, the onrushing waves push you back, slow your turn, and may even bring you to a dead stop in irons.

Secondly, as you fall away on the new tack, there is danger of capsizing if you are hit by a puff before you have full headway on again and are able to round up and spill wind. Take long tacks and come about in the lulls when the wind is comparatively light.

Handling rough and choppy seas. You will find the roughest water, with waves coming from many directions and forming a "chop," at the start of your races and whenever you have many boats together. Avoid these jams at starts and at marks. Give other boats a *wider berth* (more distance) than usual.

When beating into a strong wind, take a tack that will put you *close to shore.* Here the waves are smaller and the sea smoother. You will go faster than the boats which stay out in open water bucking the rougher waves.

11. Sailing to leeward. When on a broad reach or run, put your crew farther aft than for beating, and keep your weight up to windward in case of a knockdown puff.

Jibing. Avoid a jibe whenever possible. Even a skillful jibe is risky in heavy weather and may carry away mast and rigging. An accidental jibe most assuredly will.

To keep from jibing, do not sail directly downwind in the strong puffs. Head up a bit (Fig. 85), almost to the point of broad reaching, so you can spill a little wind and can safely keep the sail to leeward. When the puff lets up you may resume your course more directly downwind.

If it becomes absolutely necessary to change tacks, round up into the wind and come about, rather than jibe. This is called *wearing*. It is safer, but takes a little more time (Fig. 85). Keep centerboard down, even on the runs.

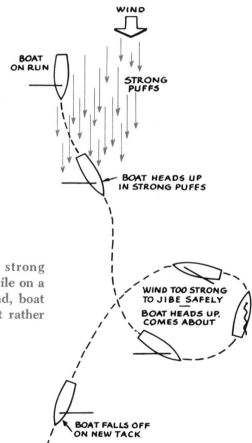

Fig. 85. Heading up in strong puffs will prevent jibing while on a run. To tack in strong wind, boat heads up and comes about rather than jibe.

Riding waves. When you find yourself on top of a wave, fall off a bit to leeward and ride the wave as long as possible. On the other hand, if you find the waves tend to bury the bow and swamp you, heading up a bit higher will usually correct this.

Planing. In centerboard boats with relatively flat bottoms, and in some smaller keel boats, additional speed can be gained on a broad reach by falling off to leeward during a puff instead of heading up to windward and luffing! The sail can actually be trimmed in more than usual, and the boat may nearly double her effective speed by skimming over the water like a hydroplane. This is called *planing*. It is to be tried only by experienced sailors, and will be discussed in Chapter 10.

SUMMARY OF HOW TO SAIL IN HEAVY WEATHER:

(1) Wear waterproof and warm clothing.
(2) Keep boat level. Sit on windward side.
(3) Don't tie sheets down. Keep halyards coiled, ready to let go. No half hitches.
(4) Tighten outhaul and downhaul. Trim sail flat.
(5) Head up in puffs.
(6) Don't tack too often. Avoid jibes.
(7) Sail in smoother water near shore.
(8) Reef sail if wind is too strong.

Fig. 86.   The eye splice.

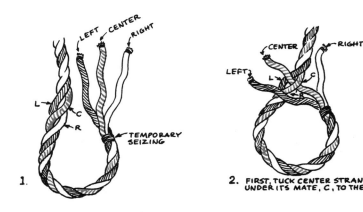

BASIC KNOTS AND SEAMANSHIP

The eye splice. (Fig. 86)

Use: To form a permanent loop in the end of a line, such as on mooring lines, anchor lines, and halyards. The splice may be formed around a metal insert, called a thimble, to prevent wear.

Splicing is as easy as basket weaving once you have started. Each strand is tucked over, under, over, under, each cross strand that it meets.

Step 1: Tie your rope with a piece of stout line about 6 inches from the end. Unlay the strands back to this tie. Put a temporary whipping on each strand.

Step 2: Spread the three strands out and bend them back toward the rope to form a loop. Have the middle strand rest on your rope (strand *C*).

Step 3: Tuck this strand *(C)* under the nearest strand of the rope, heading across the lay of the rope. Pull up fairly snug.

Step 4: Strand *L*, on your left, goes over the strand *C* went under, and goes under the next higher strand.

Step 5: Strand *R*, on your right hand, starts lower and goes under the strand just below the one *C* went under.

Step 6: Each strand is then woven for two more tucks, going over and under every other strand. Tag ends are cut off.

3. HERE THE LEFT STRAND IS TUCKED UNDER ITS MATE TO THE LEFT

4. HERE THE SPLICE IS *TURNED OVER*, AND THE RIGHT HAND STRAND IS TUCKED

5. TWO MORE TUCKS ARE MADE WITH EACH STRAND IN ROTATION. STRAND ENDS ARE CUT OFF, AND SPLICE IS NOW COMPLETED.

EXERCISES

1. Fill in the blanks:
    (a) As a general rule, when _____ appear on the water, the wind is too strong for small boat sailing.
    (b) The Coast Guard small craft warning flag is _____ in shape and _____ in color.
    (c) Personal gear for sailing in heavy weather should include _____, _____, and _____, as well as optional things like gloves and extra socks.
    (d) Sail is flattened for heavy-weather sailing by adjusting outhaul and downhaul so they are _____ than usual.
    (e) When a puff of strong wind hits, three ways to keep boat on an even keel are _____.
2. Multiple choice. Choose correct answer:
    (a) When beating, if boat tends to head up into the wind when you let go the tiller, it is called (weather helm, leeward helm, frozen helm). To correct this, you can shift weight (forward, aft, inboard).
    (b) A typical thunderhead cloud has (very little wind, a dark and "dirty bottom," fleecy white clouds at bottom).
    (c) The thunderhead can come up within (two hours, half an hour, twenty-four hours) of the time you first see it.
    (d) As a summer thunderstorm approaches, which comes first: (rain, wind, temperature drop)?
3. Check which of the following you would do in preparing for heavy weather sailing:
    (a) See that the sail has a deep pocket or belly in it.
    (b) Turn mainsheet end-for-end so fresh line is used in the places where there is most strain.
    (c) Take a reef in sail, while still at the shore.
    (d) Tie a rope to the bailing can so it isn't thrown overboard.
    (e) Wash and smooth the bottom of the boat.
4. If caught in a storm and you could not make shore, check those things you would do:
    (a) Get sails down as fast as possible.
    (b) Leave sails up and cleat the halyards so they won't slip.
    (c) Head boat into wind, and throw out a sea anchor if necessary.
    (d) Swim for shore as soon as it looked as if you could make it.
5. Give short definitions for the following:
    (a) Reef points
    (b) Luff and leach cringles
    (c) Roller reefing

(d) Storm sails

(e) Sea anchor

6. How can you use strong, puffy winds while beating?

7. What are two good reasons for sailing near the shore in heavy weather?

8. Can you safely sail directly downwind in heavy puffs? Why?

9. How can you avoid jibing in heavy weather when you have to change to the other tack?

10. Answer true or false:

(a) _____ If caught in a storm, you can sometimes run before it and make shore.

(b) _____ If caught in a storm, you may have to take down sail at once.

(c) _____ A falling barometer means bad weather may be coming.

(d) _____ Sheets are never cleated in heavy weather.

(e) _____ Halyards are locked with half hitches to keep from slipping in strong winds.

(f) _____ A boat usually sails faster on an even keel in strong winds.

(g) _____ The weather report says there will be a fresh breeze, with winds at 17 to 21 knots; therefore, there will be no whitecaps.

(h) _____ A wet, windy day first thing in the morning may be clear by noon.

(i) _____ Pulling sheet more *down* than *in* helps to flatten sail.

(j) _____ In heavy weather you will come about faster if crew sits up in bow and you sit well aft in stern.

PRACTICE DRILL

1. Each day that you come to the water, try to determine by looking at waves, trees and boats sailing, what the strength of the wind is for that day. Write it down in knots or miles per hour. At the end of the day or week, check your local paper and see how close you were. You might even check with your local weather bureau or airport for a quicker report. This will teach you good judgment of wind.

2. Borrow, buy or observe a barometer. Watch it each day and keep a record, noting whether that day is cloudy or bright, and what the wind conditions are. Note cloud formations. Your library probably has a book with pictures of clouds and what they mean. Become a weather expert.

3. For practice, wear a life jacket during your next race.

4. If your boat has reef points, or if you can find one that does, practice putting in a reef, sail with it, then shake it out. Only by practicing this on shore or at the dock can you put one in when you are being blown about at sea.

5. On a practice sail when winds are fairly strong, haul in the sheet and let the boat heel. Now ease the sheet and notice the increase in speed as the boat levels. If you have any heavy weather, keep the boat level and sail with a luff if necessary.

8. Sailing in Light Weather

Most sailors complain more about sailing in light winds than in heavy, and rightly so. Wind is your motor. As it dies down, sailing becomes more and more difficult . . . until the point where there is no wind at all and you are becalmed.

There are a good many tricks to sailing in light wind, and ways to make your boat go when there seems to be no wind at all.

1. Trim and set of sails. When the wind is light ("light airs"), you need a great deal of curve to the belly or airfoil of your sail. And you can use bigger sails. If you own a sail that is light in weight, large, and baggy — that is, one having a deep pocket or belly — use it in light weather. If you have only one sail, shape it to fit. Here is how.

Outhauls and downhauls. Keep these slack in light wind, and the sail will belly out in the middle. But keep them just tight enough so that large wrinkles are kept out of the sail.

The boom and sheet. As we learned in the last chapter, anything that pulls downward on the sail tends to flatten it. This includes the boom and the heavy fittings on it. For light winds the heavy-duty blocks may be changed for lighter ones, and a heavy sheet replaced by a lighter one. Nylon or other synthetic lines are ideal since they give added strength for less weight.

On some boats you may be able to reeve (pass or thread) your sheet differently so it goes through fewer blocks (pulleys). This cuts down weight and friction, lets the sheet slack more easily, and allows the boom to lift and give more fullness to the sail.

Since the angle of pull of the mainsheet will change the shape of the sail, you should move your deck block inboard (Fig. 87) if it is adjustable. If not, you can simply hold the sheet in your hand and not trim through a block at all.

2. Trim of boat. In light weather your boat needs to heel. This helps the sail billow out naturally and allows it to take advantage of

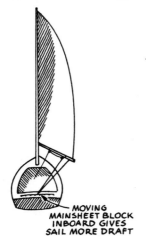

MOVING
MAINSHEET BLOCK
INBOARD GIVES
SAIL MORE DRAFT

Fig. 87.   Increasing fullness of sail by bringing angle of sheet more inboard.

the lightest winds. Sometimes both you and your crew must sit to leeward (Fig. 88), and this heeling may be very extreme. Some boats just plain sail better in light wind when they are over on their chine (the edge where side and bottom meet).

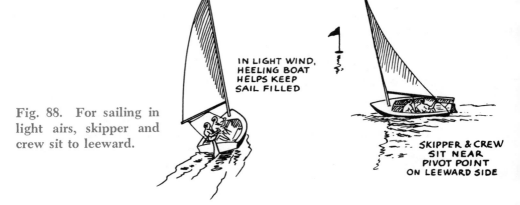

IN LIGHT WIND,
HEELING BOAT
HELPS KEEP
SAIL FILLED

Fig. 88.   For sailing in light airs, skipper and crew sit to leeward.

SKIPPER & CREW
SIT NEAR
PIVOT POINT
ON LEEWARD SIDE

Position in boat. Sitting near the pivot point is even more important in light airs. It is a known principle of physics that a spinning object will turn faster if most of its weight is close to the center, or pivot point. If you and your crew sit at far ends of your boat, you will turn more slowly and in light winds may not have the power to turn all the way about!

3. Effect of waves. When it is very calm and your sails are hardly filled, keep a sharp eye out for passing motor boats. Waves from these will make your boat roll and can shake the wind right out of the sail. The best you can do to counteract this is to have your crew steady the boom and head your boat temporarily into the waves. You will roll less if you meet the waves head on.

4. Special duties of crew. The biggest job of the crew is to sit quietly in the boat. Nothing is worse in light weather than a crew member who moves around ponderously, rocking the boat, shaking the sail, and knocking out what little wind and speed you may have.

Crew should sit low, as anything sticking up in the boat interferes with the wind currents and will decrease the force of wind on the sail. From a position low in the cockpit, crew can reach an arm up to steady the boom when waves approach, or when you come about, or when you are running downwind. A gentle push forward on the boom when you are running will put tension on the sheet and keep it from dragging in the water.

5. How to make your boat go faster. The first thing to do is make sure you have nothing dragging behind — lines, sheets, seaweed on the rudder, hands and feet! Over a mile course downwind in light airs, a rope dragging in the water can easily slow you two or more boat lengths behind a competing boat.

Every part of the boat that touches the water makes friction with the water. Friction slows the boat. For this reason the hull must be as smooth and clean as possible. Clean off all barnacles and other marine life. Clean off sea grass and moss. Use a fine grade of waterproof sandpaper and go over your bottom lightly. Lastly, use a sponge or flannel cloth and wash it down with soap and water. All of this except the last can be done with your boat in the water, but is easiest if the boat is hauled out.

Rudder and centerboard. In cleaning your hull, don't neglect the rudder, skeg, centerboard and centerboard well. To reduce drag, the edges of the rudder and centerboard should be streamlined by filing and sanding them to a rounded shape. They should never be sharpened to a point. The rudder should fit as close to the skeg as possible to keep an even flow of water going by without eddies.

Foot, don't pinch. In light airs don't try to sail as close to the wind as you can in stronger wind. This is pinching, and it won't work. Instead, *start your sheets* (let them out a little), so sail is not pulled in tightly. You will foot faster through the water and this extra speed will more than make up for the longer distance sailed. This is one of the most important things to remember about sailing to windward in light weather.

6. Anchoring in current. In light winds, where the breeze is uncertain, current and tide are much less important than on a day when the wind is steadier and stronger. The exception is when the current is stronger than the wind and pushes you backward.

When this happens it is time to anchor. It is legal to do so in races, as long as you don't move your boat ahead or back with the anchor. Many a boat has lost a race because the tide moved her backward when she should have anchored. When the wind picks up, raise anchor and sail off.

7. Signs of new wind. Instead of worrying about tides or currents, or much about other boats in your race, you should be concerned primarily with the weather.

Most hot, still, cloudless days have no wind. Smoke from a chimney goes straight up. There are not enough little zephyrs even to ripple the water. This kind of day is called a *drifter*. Here the sailor's chief concern is new wind. There are many clues to tell you where it is.

(a) *Smoke moving on shore.* A puff of smoke on shore moving in a new direction tells of fresh wind. If the smoke from a chimney is high, it means the wind is high. But chances are it will settle down on the water, anyway.

(b) *Look for clouds.* Where there are clouds there is wind. Even the fluffy cumulus clouds of a hot summer day bring wind. In an afternoon they may even merge together and build up into a thunderhead!

(c) *Watch other boats.* If boats at a distance fill away on a new tack, it means they have fresh wind. Before you sail after them, however, see that it is a steady wind and not just a passing puff.

(d) *Head for dark water.* Streaks of dark water near shore or horizon mean fresh wind. Have your crew keep on the alert for these, and when they start to build up, try to get there first.

(e) *Play the shore.* Every body of water has a different shore line, and the winds will be different. If you have high cliffs they may catch high winds and funnel them down to the water. Get near and see. If there are rivers or gorges that empty along the shore, they also may act like a funnel for small breezes. But if fresh wind is expected, don't get caught too near cliffs and shore, as the wind will be stronger out in the open water.

(f) *Land and sea breezes.* In many areas there will be an afternoon breeze coming from the sea toward the land (*sea breeze*). In the evening this will change to a wind coming off the shore (*offshore*, or *land breeze*). Here's why this happens.

Water stays at a pretty constant temperature. Land heats up during the day and cools rapidly at night. If the land is warmer than the water, air rises over it and pulls air in from over the water. This is a sea breeze and comes up in mid-afternoon until dusk. As the sun goes down, the land cools more than the water. Now the air rises over the water and the breeze comes offshore.

(g) *The rising barometer.* The barometer will rise for northerly winds and fair weather. If the rise is rapid, expect strong winds. If the rise is very slow from a low point, again expect strong winds.

8. Tacking. In light winds, with breezes coming from "all over the lot" and from nowhere in particular, tack only to stay in a wind puff. Every time you tack you lose headway and wind, so do it as little as possible. When coming about, turn slowly. If you put the tiller way over to one side, the rudder will act like a drag and slow you down more than turn the boat. On the other hand, in jibing, the crew can pull the sail in rapidly since this extra push against the wind will send the boat ahead faster. But let the sail out slowly on the other side so it doesn't backwind and act as a brake. Keep centerboard up when running.

SUMMARY OF HOW TO SAIL IN LIGHT WEATHER:

(1) Loosen outhaul and downhaul. Use large, baggy sail.
(2) Pull in, not down, on sail to let the boom lift and give sail more fullness.
(3) Sit to leeward. Let boat heel.
(4) Keep sheets and lines out of water.
(5) On a beat, let sheet out a few inches. Foot, don't pinch.
(6) Sail toward new winds.
(7) Come about slowly. Tack as little as possible.
(8) Use lightweight sheets.

BASIC KNOTS AND SEAMANSHIP

The short splice. (Fig. 89)

Use: For joining two ropes together, provided they do not have to run through a block. The short splice is stronger than any knot.

When the splice is completed, roll it on deck under foot to make it smoother, then trim off the ends.

Step 1: Tie stout cord around each line about 6 inches from the end. Unravel each rope and tie each strand.

Step 2: "Marry" the two ropes by bringing together the strands from each one alternating with the other.

Step 3: Tie all strands of one rope temporarily to the other.

Step 4: Tuck each strand over and under, working across the lay of the rope. When finished with one side, cut the temporary tie and do the others.

Step 5: Take two or three tucks with each strand on each side. Trim ends, but leave half an inch sticking up so ends don't pull through.

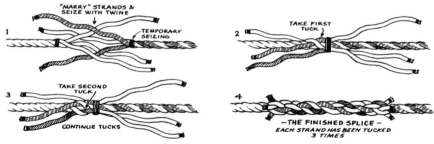

Fig. 89. Short splice.

EXERCISES

QUESTIONS

1. Put an *L* (for light wind) or an *S* (for strong wind) before the following items, indicating which wind they are best suited for. Some items have both *L* and *S*.

   (a) _____ Baggy, curved, deep-bellied sail.

   (b) _____ Slack outhauls and downhauls.

   (c) _____ Flat, old, blown-out sail.

   (d) _____ Crew and skipper sit to leeward.

   (e) _____ Crew and skipper sit near pivot point.

   (f) _____ Take mainsheet out of block, or move traveler block inboard.

   (g) _____ Use smaller sail of heavier canvas.

   (h) _____ Sail boat as level as possible in the water.

   (i) _____ Never cleat the sheets.

2. In light weather it is important that nothing be dragging from the boat. Name three things that might drag.

3. Friction on the hull slows the boat. Before sailing in light weather, go over the hull with _____and finish by washing with_____ .

4. Why is it important to start the sheets, and not pinch, in light weather?

5. When in light-weather sailing might you use the anchor?_____ Is it permitted? _____

6. You are sailing in a drifter and just barely moving. List five ways you might try to find new wind.

7. Answer true or false:

    (a) _____ A rising barometer generally means rain.

    (b) _____ In light airs it is best to tack often to catch every little puff.

    (c) _____ Come about slowly in light winds.

    (d) _____ Pull sail in rapidly when jibing in light winds.

    (e) _____ Keep centerboard down when running.

    (f) _____ Afternoon and evening breezes usually blow off the land toward the water.

    (g) _____ High buildings near shore may funnel high winds down to the water.

    (h) _____ Fresh winds are apt to be stronger out in the lake, rather than close to shore, especially if there are many hills or cliffs.

    (i) _____ Rudder and centerboard should be filed to a sharp edge, rather than rounded, to cut through the water faster.

PRACTICE DRILL

1. Review previous racing rules, in preview of next chapter.

2. Sail around a triangular course following another boat (or line of boats, if in a sailing class). Notice how the lead boat generally pulls away from the others behind (this will be discussed in later chapters). Have the leader sail an obstacle course around moorings, moored boats, docks, etc. By now you should be able to maneuver clear of all of these things. If not, give them plenty of room when you tack.

3. After this follow-the-leader series, sail in as many races as possible. But this time, try to avoid being directly behind a leading boat. You have seen that it doesn't work out.

4. When wind is light, use all the techniques of sailing in light airs. Take along a pair of binoculars if you can. Tie them to the boat with a piece of cord. Use them to search the shoreline and horizon for signs of new wind.

5. On a cooling summer night, before it gets dark, take a short sail and see if you can pick up an evening offshore breeze. These are often gentle winds which allow you to reach up and back the shore. It is a good time to practice sailing in light airs. Take a flashlight and don't sail too far from shore!

9. Starting Your Race

The start of a race is the most exciting part, the most difficult, and also the most important. A boat with a good start is hard to beat in any race. If you race at all, you must learn to be a good starter.

The difficulty at the start is that boats are crowded together, skippers and crews are keyed up, the water is choppy from the wakes of many boats, and the wind is deflected from sail to sail and unpredictable. To make things easier, certain rules have been set up and certain starting tactics are recommended.

1. Rules at the start. There are two basic rules at the start that you must know.

(1) *Over line early rule:* A boat that is on the wrong side of the starting line at the start signal must give way to all other boats.

This means that if you cross the line before the gun, or if you are on the wrong side of the line to begin with when the gun goes off, you must keep clear of all other boats (Fig. 90).

Even if you are a starboard tack boat, the port tack boats that

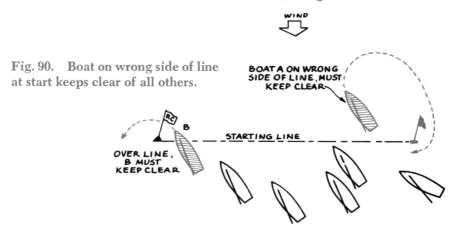

Fig. 90.   Boat on wrong side of line at start keeps clear of all others.

are starting correctly have right of way over you. You have to get back and restart. Once you do, the other racing rules apply as before.

(2) *Anti-barging rule:* A boat close-hauled at the starting line does NOT have to give room between itself and the mark to an overlapped boat.

At other marks of the course a boat with an overlap is allowed buoy room, that is, room to round the mark. But this does not apply at the start (Fig. 91).

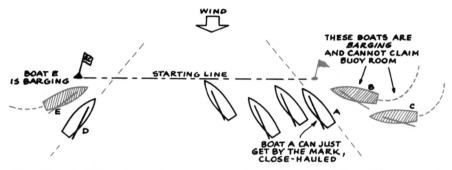

Fig. 91. Anti-barging rule prevents a boat from claiming "buoy room" at either end of starting line.

Boats trying to get buoy room here are said to be *barging.* It is not permitted. If you are close-hauled and can just pass the mark, no one can slip in between you and the mark.

2. Methods of starting. There are four different methods of starting your race. One method is good, the other three are poor. Your objective in starting is not only to be at the line just as the gun sounds, but also to be sailing across in the proper direction *with full headway.* Only in this way can you steer and outmaneuver your competitor.

(a) *Sitting on line.* In this method you sail up to the starting line with a minute or two to go, let your sail luff, and wait for the gun (Fig. 92).

But what happens at the start signal? You trim in your sail and try to get underway, but this takes time. Boats go by on each side, stealing your wind, rocking your boat with their wakes, and you will be lucky to get started in the next few minutes after they are gone.

(b) **Running the line.** This is a favorite method for beginners and for those who haven't taken the trouble to time their start. It is somewhat similar to the first method (Fig. 92).

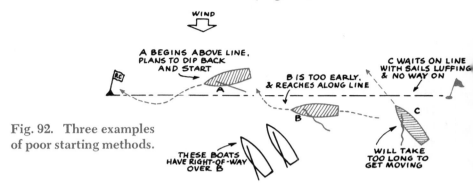

Fig. 92. Three examples
of poor starting methods.

Here you sail along the starting line during the last minute or half minute before the start, and plan to trim sheets and head up and cross the line just at the start signal. If it takes a full minute to sail the length of the starting line you may begin at one end with thirty seconds to go and hope to start about the middle.

Disadvantages. First, if the wind picks up you may reach along the line faster than you counted on. To slow down you luff your sail and spill wind. This makes it harder to steer and maneuver.

Second, it is hard to tell if you are on the wrong side of the line when you are out in the middle portion of it. Third, boats approaching the line below you have the right of way, since you are the windward boat. They may force you to head up into the wind and may even force you over the line early!

Sometimes this starting method is used when a boat arrives at the line too early and must use up ten or twenty seconds without going over the starting line. If there are not many boats below you, this may work to your advantage.

(c) **Approaching above the line.** Here you actually begin by staying above the starting line (on the side nearest the next mark of the course). You keep clear of other boats and try and sail down to dip across the line and back just as the gun sounds (Fig. 92).

Disadvantages. Again, you are windward boat of most of the others and they have right of way over you, unless a port and starboard tack situation applies. If the wind drops and you are unable to get down to the line before the start begins, you have no rights at all. Also, if the starting line is crowded with leeward boats, you may not have room to sail between them or turn around.

In races where there is a long starting line and few boats are at the part where you choose to start, this method can work, although it is not recommended.

(d) *Timed start, close-hauled.* This is the most widely accepted starting method. Here you choose that part of the line you wish to cross and which tack to be on (usually starboard tack so you have right of way). Next, you sail back and forth across the line enough times so you know about how fast you can sail in the wind and how long it takes to come about from a run to a beat (Fig. 93).

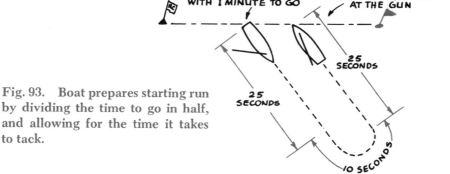

Fig. 93. Boat prepares starting run by dividing the time to go in half, and allowing for the time it takes to tack.

When this is done, you plan your starting run. Pick the place on the line where you hope to start. At a few minutes before the start you sail across this place, going away from the line. Let's say you have four and a half minutes to go. You know it takes half a minute to change from run to beat, so this allows four minutes to go down and back. By sailing below the line for two minutes, turning in half a minute, and coming back up in two minutes, you should be at the start just about on time.

If your boat is large, your starting run may be five or ten minutes long. On the other hand, in a small dinghy it may only be for one or two minutes, since small boats are more easily maneuvered.

(e) *Multiple-pass method.* This is a variation of the timed start, and is used by experts in small boat racing. Choose the point on the line where you wish to start. Sail across line close-hauled at this point.

As you approach the line, look dead astern and line up an object ashore, such as a tree, smokestack, barn, etc. This object we'll call your *range marker*. After you have sailed over the line and beyond it for half a minute, turn around and run back, heading directly for your range marker. In this way you are sailing on the same course each time you practice the start (Fig. 94). Now to time it.

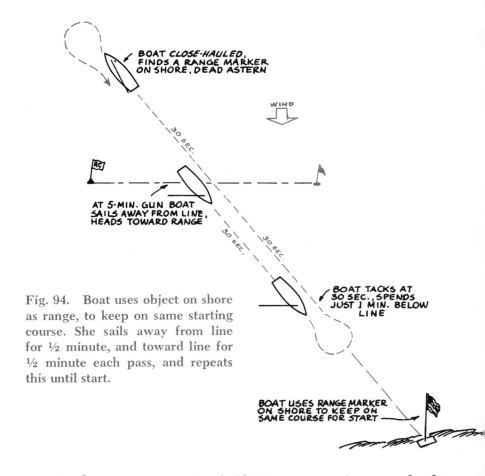

Fig. 94. Boat uses object on shore as range, to keep on same starting course. She sails away from line for ½ minute, and toward line for ½ minute each pass, and repeats this until start.

At the preparatory signal (five-minute gun), cross the line toward your range marker at the place you have chosen. Sail below the line for half a minute, subtracting a few seconds for the start of your turn. Then head up on a beat over the same course, keeping the range marker dead astern. Continue for half a minute above the line, a total of one full minute on the beat, then turn and sail back toward the range. Keep repeating this. You should cross the starting line exactly on the minutes (Fig. 94) and make your turns on the half-minutes. If not, you can shorten or lengthen the next leg of your run as necessary.

This is the experts' method of getting a well-practiced start in good position. Timing it is most important. Because you will be busy with the boat, it may be easier to have crew handle watch and timing.

Crew's duties in counting time to go. When the warning signal for your race is given, crew must be alert, watch for the signal, and start the watch.

The watch is started at the instant the flag or other signal is hoisted, or when the puff of smoke from the gun is seen, whichever is first (theoretically they will occur at same time). Remember, light travels faster than sound, so you will see the smoke and flash of the gun seconds before you will hear it. Therefore, remember, start your watch — and your race — when the signal is hoisted, not when you hear the sound!

Until the preparatory signal your crew will call out each minute as follows: "Nine minutes to go . . . eight minutes to go . . ." etc. Or he may say: "Four minutes to preparatory signal . . ." etc.

One-half minute before the next signal, he checks the watch and calls, "Flag down," when the signal is lowered. If his timing is off, he should stop the watch and restart it with the preparatory signal which is coming up in thirty seconds.

Counting time in last five minutes. After the preparatory signal most skippers want their crews to count off the time more frequently, such as every half minute: "Five minutes to go . . . four and a half minutes to go . . ." etc. With one minute left, they can count every ten seconds: "Fifty seconds to go . . . forty seconds to go . . . thirty seconds . . ." etc. In the last ten seconds they should count each one: "10, 9, 8, 7, 6, 5, 4, 3, 2, 1, START!" If your timing is correct, the start signal is up, the gun sounds, and you are off!

By letting your crew do the timing, you are free to maneuver and keep track of your distance and heading without being distracted by looking at your watch. Crew counts out the last minute so you can hear the exact time in these crucial moments before the start.

SUMMARY OF TIPS ON TIMING YOUR START:

(1) Practice sailing across line at point where you wish to start.

(2) Use a range marker to stay on course.

(3) Time your practice runs exactly.

(4) Start watch at ten minutes to go, check at five minutes to go.

(5) Have crew sound off time to go.

3. Tactics. Where to start on line. We will discuss windward starts only. The line has certain designations (Fig. 95). As you head across it to windward, the end on your right is the starboard end, and on your left is the port end. Because so many boats start on starboard tack, the starboard end is often referred to as the windward end, since it is on your windward side. The other is the leeward end.

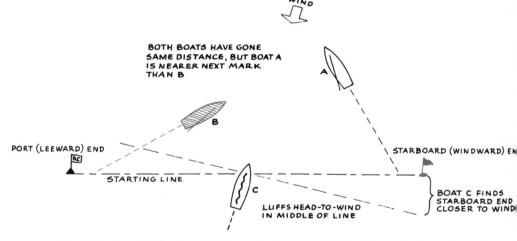

Fig. 95.   Boat luffs directly into wind near middle of line, finds starboard end is closer to wind.

Perfect starting line. The ideal line is set at right angles to the wind and at right angles to the direction of the next mark.

If a boat started at one end of the line on port tack and at the other end of the line on starboard tack, they would meet after traveling exactly the same distance. This is the fairest start, and one which race committees hope to achieve to give all boats an equal change on the line.

Favored end of line. Many times, however, one end of the line is favored. This means it is closer to the wind than the other, and to your advantage to start there.

To find out which end is favored, test the line by luffing dead into the wind in the middle of the line. If one end is more upwind than the other, it is favored. Boats starting here (Fig. 95), traveling the same distance as boats from the other end, will be ahead and well up to windward when their courses cross.

When the port end is favored (Fig. 96), boats at this end will probably be able to cross the starboard tack boats from the other

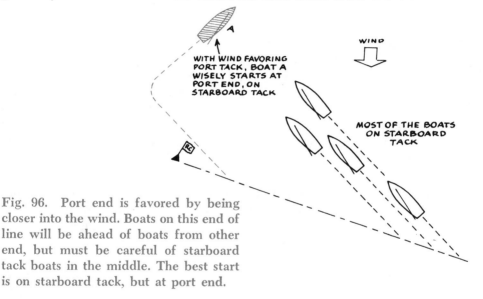

WITH WIND FAVORING PORT TACK, BOAT A WISELY STARTS AT PORT END, ON STARBOARD TACK

WIND

MOST OF THE BOATS ON STARBOARD TACK

Fig. 96. Port end is favored by being closer into the wind. Boats on this end of line will be ahead of boats from other end, but must be careful of starboard tack boats in the middle. The best start is on starboard tack, but at port end.

end safely. However, boats in the central parts of the line may not be able to do so and should be ready to come about to give way.

When the starting line is crowded, it may be difficult to start at the port end (leeward end) of the line *on the port tack*. This brings up another consideration.

Which tack at start. The starboard tack is preferred at the start to give you right of way. It is very difficult to try and thread your way through a fleet of starboard tack boats while you are on port tack and must give every one of them right of way.

Suppose the port end of the line is favored, and you want to make a "leeward end start." If it looks as if there will be many starboard tack boats along the line, it is best for you to join them, but be in position down at the leeward end and come about on the favoring port tack as soon after the start as you can (Fig. 96).

When to start on port tack. There are two times when it is advisable to start on port tack. One is when the port end is strongly favored and there are few boats at this end of the line. The other is when nearly every boat is starting on port tack for an obviously favored wind. Here it is unwise, and probably unsportsmanlike, to try and "starboard tack" the entire fleet — although it is perfectly legal to do so.

Avoid crowds at start. There is a tendency among junior sailors and beginners to start at the same part of the line where everybody else does. This is usually at the windward end of the line on starboard tack. It happens so often that race committees many times set a line that favors the port end, just to get boats to move down to leeward!

If you get caught in a jam at the start, you will find the wind is bounced from sail to sail and is undependable, there are waves and wake from boats which make steering difficult, and all in all you have a poor start. So pick your own spot, look for your opening between the other boats, and avoid crowds — unless, of course, you are very skillful, in which case you can try the windward end on starboard tack with the others.

The late start. When arriving so late after the start that there are few if any boats near the line, start on either tack and sail only that course which will head you closest to the next mark. But remember, you have to sail over the starting line before you do so.

Maintaining headway. One of the most important things at the start is to have full headway. If you are going full speed ahead when the start is made, you will get clear of other boats and get an earlier lead that will be hard to beat.

Maintaining headway is not always easy. If the wind strengthens, you will go faster and arrive at the line too soon, and have to luff sail to kill your headway (Fig. 97). However, if you luff *before* getting to the line, you can trim sheets in the last ten or fifteen seconds and start with full headway.

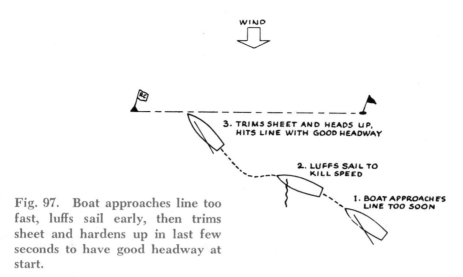

WIND

3. TRIMS SHEET AND HEADS UP, HITS LINE WITH GOOD HEADWAY

2. LUFFS SAIL TO KILL SPEED

1. BOAT APPROACHES LINE TOO SOON

Fig. 97. Boat approaches line too fast, luffs sail early, then trims sheet and hardens up in last few seconds to have good headway at start.

4. What to do if over line early. Good starters are said to be over the line early once in every six or seven starts. This is because they are eager all the time to be early enough. So if you are over too soon, don't worry. Obey the rules.

First, keep clear of all other boats that have started. Even if you are starboard tack and they are port, you keep clear. Second, start your race again as soon as you can. If there are many boats near you, tack for the nearest end of the line and swing around the starting mark on a new start. If there are no boats near you, fall off at once and dip across the line and back again on a fresh start.

Whatever you do, don't give up. Some races have been won by the boat that started late — and your habit of being early will pay off with good starts in your other races!

BASIC KNOTS AND SEAMANSHIP

Hanging a coil.

Use: On yachts over the 20-foot length, halyards are usually coiled and hung on the halyard cleat. Sheets can be hung in a coil when boat is not in use. Yachts with two or three masts and many sails may have a *pin rail* on which lines are coiled and hung over a *belaying pin.* Hanging a coil properly is a simple but neat trick and helps make a good seaman of a fair sailor.

Step 1: The coil is made up (coiled) starting at the cleat and working toward the free end.
Step 2: Hold coil in left hand, about 8 or 12 inches from cleat. Reach through coil with right hand and grasp the part of the line coming from the cleat.
Step 3: Pull this out under the coil, put one or two twists in it, and hook these over the top horn of the cleat.

Securing rope for storage.

Use: When manila line is put away, it should be hung up on something, such as a wooden peg, where it will stay dry. Here is a way to keep stored lines shipshape.

Step 1: Coil right-laid rope in a clockwise direction.
Step 2: Tie coil at three or four places with light cotton twine which will break easily when coil is to be used.

EXERCISES

QUESTIONS

1. What is barging?
2. What is the anti-barging rule?
   Does it ever apply anywhere except at the start?_____. Does it apply at the start after the start signal is given?_____.
3. What is the over line early rule?
   Does it apply to boats that were never on the right side of the starting line to begin with?_____.
4. Here is your start. The gun has just gone off and the race begins (Fig. 98). Black in all boats which must keep clear. Write down the rule which applies.

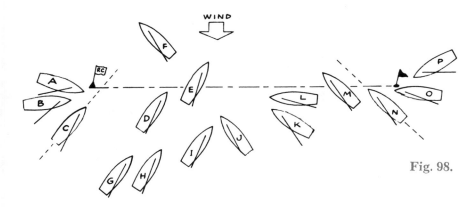

Fig. 98.

5. Multiple choice. Choose the best answer:
   (a) It is best at the start to (have full headway, to be on time and have sails luffing, to sit on line with no headway).
   (b) Reaching along the starting line is not good if there are (boats to windward of you, boats to leeward of you, boats barging).
   (c) With fifteen seconds to go, the wind picks up and you are approaching the line too fast. It is best to (luff sail now to slow down, keep sailing to line and then luff sail, fall off to leeward).
   (d) The boat next to you has crossed the line too soon, and the gun goes off. You should (give it room to get back across line, give it room only if you are port tack boat, sail your own race and let it give *you* room).
   (e) You are making a run before the start and are sailing away from the line with two minutes to go. The wind is getting lighter and lighter. You should (make your run longer, make your run shorter, allow fewer seconds for turning).

6. What is the advantage of having a range marker at the start? How do you use it?

7. What is a favored end of the starting line? How do you find it?

8. Answer true or false:
   (a) _____ Since most boats start at the windward end of the line (starboard end), barging is permitted at the port end.
   (b) _____ Crossing the line on starboard tack is preferred.
   (c) _____ The favored end of the line is more to windward than the other end.
   (d) _____ When boats are crowded together at the start, there are more waves and the wind is less strong.
   (e) _____ If you are over the line early every few races, you are a "poor starter."
   (f) _____ If you approach the line too fast, you can sometimes slow down by heading up into the wind and luffing.

(g) _____ If you have to slow down, it is better to do it before you get within three or four boat lengths from the start, rather than after.

(h) _____ The favored end may not have much advantage if there are a great many boats starting there.

(i) _____ A boat over the line early is at least allowed room to tack by other boats, so he can get back to line and start.

PRACTICE DRILL

1. Again, do your practice work on shore first before setting out in your boat. Set your model boats up on a table. Use any convenient objects to represent the starting line (salt and pepper shakers, corks, etc.). Draw a chalk line along the starting line and another for the wind direction, or use your fan.

   Set up the two boats in various positions to show the racing rules at the start. Get so you can tell the boats' positions at a glance — what tack each is on, where the wind is, what the boats' headings are — and know the rule which applies for that position. Test your crew, then have him set the boats up and test you.

2. Using the models on a table, set up a triangular racing course and put the boats in various positions. Test your skill in knowing which rule governs the boats in each case, then check your answer with the book.

3. Review Chapter 6, Section 3, "How you start your race," so you know the official starting signals and colors. If there is any question about the starting signals where you race, ask the race committee before you go out next time.

4. Practice starts. To be a good starter you have to be able to sail your boat a specific distance (up to the starting line) over a definite and limited period of time (the minutes and seconds to go). This ability only comes with long practice.

   Set up two buoys so they are a few boat lengths apart, and form a line running across the wind (for a windward start). Practice sailing across this line with a prearranged time to go for your start. One way to do this is to borrow a small oven timer from your kitchen . . . the kind you can set to ring a bell at the end of any number of minutes. Take this with you on the boat (if you can), set it for one, two, three, or even five minutes, and try to make a timed start by the time the bell sounds. The timer is not as accurate as your watch, so don't worry about missing the line by a few seconds. If you can get someone ashore to blow a starting whistle, so much the better.

5. Try different starting methods while racing. Each time you race, try a different method of timing the start, and try to start at various positions on the line. If you start one race at the windward end, try the next one at the leeward end. Notice that a starboard tack start just at the leeward end of the line is difficult — especially if you are a bit early.

6. In every starting drill, attempt to be over the line early. This is not as easy as it sounds. Most boats are five to twenty seconds late for a start, in the smaller classes, and if you are watching the bunch you will be just as late. Start in front . . . and stay in front!

CHECK LIST OF BASIC SKILLS*

You have now completed Part I. The material in this part is so presented that if you know it thoroughly, you are a qualified sailing skipper. This means you are capable of taking out a boat under your own command and sailing it or racing it properly — to the credit of yourself and your club.

These are the basic skills that you need to know to be qualified as a sailing skipper.

I. Recognition of parts of catboat hull, rigging, and sail

1. Mast	7. Tiller	13. Head	19. Telltales
2. Boom	8. Centerboard	14. Tack	20. Bow chock
3. Stays	9. Trunk	15. Clew	21. Halyard
4. Shrouds	10. Sheet	16. Luff	22. Cleats
5. Gooseneck	11. Downhaul	17. Leach	23. Blocks
6. Rudder	12. Outhaul	18. Foot	24. Turnbuckles

II. Recognition of terms dealing with actions of boats

1. Headway, sternway, leeway	5. Pivot point
2. Wake, track of disturbance	6. Launching, landing, mooring
3. Heading up, falling off	7. Tacking
4. Heeling, capsizing	8. Jibing

III. Recognition of terms dealing with lines and anchors

1. Sheet	6. Cast off	11. Make fast
2. Heaving line	7. Ease sheet	12. Scope
3. Securing	8. Harden sheet	13. Anchor line
4. Reeve	9. Pay out	14. Fender
5. Bend	10. Fouled, clear	

IV. Basic knots and seamanship

1. Cleating	8. Whipping a line
2. Square knot	9. Eye splice
3. Figure-8 knot	10. Short splice
4. Round turn and two half hitches	11. Hanging a coil
5. Clove hitch	12. Coiling down and leaving clear for running
6. Bowline	13. Securing rope for storage
7. Heaving a line	

* As adapted from a check list of basic skills devised by Mr. Ed Hulek, sailing instructor of the Rochester Yacht Club, Rochester, New York.

V. Recognition of wind, boat, and sail directions

1. Close-hauled	6. Running free	11. Abeam
2. Beating	7. Luffing	12. On the bow
3. Close reaching	8. In irons	13. On the quarter
4. Beam reaching	9. Ahead	14. To leeward
5. Broad reaching	10. Astern	15. To windward

VI. Recognition of orders given in small boats

1. Stand by to tack, stand by to come about, ready about
2. Hard alee
3. Stand by to jibe, ready to jibe
4. Jibe ho, jibing over
5. Falling off, hardening up

VII. Recognition of basic safety factors

1. Ability to swim	6. What to do if capsized
2. Use of life jackets	7. Towing procedure
3. Safe load	8. Dangerous wind or weather
4. Bailers	9. Mouth-to-mouth breathing
5. Paddles	technique

VIII. Basic seamanship problems

1. Rig catboat, launch, and get ready for sailing
2. Secure boat for night
3. Tie boat at dock; show care of hull, sails and rigging
4. Sail as crew under qualified skipper; respond to all orders and maneuvers, including tacking and jibing
5. Sail as skipper, give orders and directions to crew
6. Make landings at dock as directed
7. Luff to a mooring; get in irons and out of irons
8. Perform basic maneuvers: jibe, come about; change from beat to run, run to beat, run or beat to reach
9. Reef, if reefing gear is available
10. Sail a short course around markers, as directed

IX. Recognition of right of way

1. Opposite tack rule	4. Tacking and jibing rule
2. Same tack rule	5. Rules at the start
3. Overlapping at marks	6. Avoiding collisions

PART II

INTERMEDIATE
SAILING
AND RACING

In Part I we learned the basic elements of sailing and racing, using the one-sail catboat as our guide. In Part II we are going to move up in the sailing world and try our hand in the larger Marconi-rigged sloop.

This type of rig, with two triangular sails, is the most popular in the world and accounts for by far the greatest number of class boats. All the principles of sailing we have learned will apply here as well, but there are some new techniques and new rigging to know about.

Anyone aspiring to be a competent sailor or yachtsman must have a thorough understanding of small boat sailing and how to handle a sloop.

10. Sailing the Sloop

A sloop is rigged with one mast and two sails, the larger sail being aft and called the *mainsail* (mains'l). When both sails become nearly equal in size and the mast is more toward the middle, the rig is a *cutter*.

The mainsail may be a four-sided sail with a *gaff* (an upper boom) to support it, making the boat a gaff-rigged sloop. When the mainsail is triangular it is *jib-headed*, or *Marconi-rigged*. Years ago it was found that these tall, thin sails were much faster than the shorter four-sided ones, so the Marconi rig grew greatly in popularity.

The sloop hull is basically the same as that of the catboat, although it may have more deck. Typical class boats are the Snipe, Comet, Star, Thistle, Blue Jay and Lightning. These range from 15 to 23 feet in length, and are designed for fast racing and easy upkeep. It is from these highly competitive boats that some of the world's best racing skippers emerge.

1. Nomenclature of the sloop. These larger boats require more rigging and sails . . . and more knowledge to handle. The large sloop mast is under additional strain with the jib, so supporting stays and shrouds are added (Fig. 99).

Headstays, jumper stays, jibstays. The *jibstay* runs about three quarters of the way to the top of the mast and supports the jib. The stay should be kept as tight as possible, otherwise the jib sags off to leeward and reduces the boat's speed. This is a good thing to remember, and will be discussed later.

To support the top of the mast, most sloops have either a *headstay* running to the head of the mast, or a *jumper stay*. The jumper has a strut for support, and can be adjusted only when the mast is down. The headstay adjusts from the deck.

Shrouds and diamonds. For support sideways (athwartships),

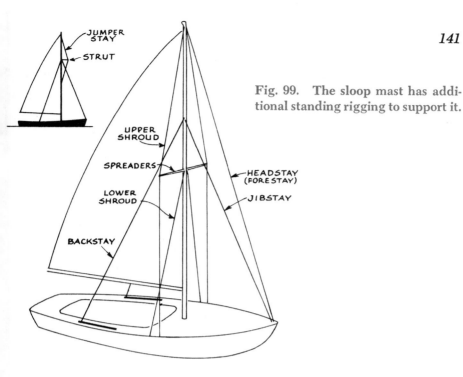

upper shrouds and spreaders, or a rig of shrouds which looks like a diamond, are added (Fig. 99). Shrouds and stays are kept tight by means of turnbuckles at the deck or on the mast.

Adjustable backstays. Most sloops have some sort of adjustable or movable backstay which gives support to the mast from astern. There are two, one on the port side and one on starboard. When the boom and sail are over a particular side, that backstay is slacked while the other is taut.

Some classes, such as the Lightnings, have a fixed or permanent backstay which attaches to the stern and is clear of the sail and boom. Snipes and some classes of dinghies have no backstays at all, but have heavier masts and rigging to take up the added strain.

How backstays are adjusted. There are only two positions for the stays: *tight*, or on; and *slack*, or off. The slack position allows the stay to be moved well forward so it does not cut the sail or boom when they swing out to that side.

There are three devices commonly used to slack the backstay: a running track, levers, and a rope pulley system (block and tackle). Levers and tracks are used on the majority of the racing classes, while the block and tackle backstays are used on larger sloops and ocean-cruising yachts (Fig. 100).

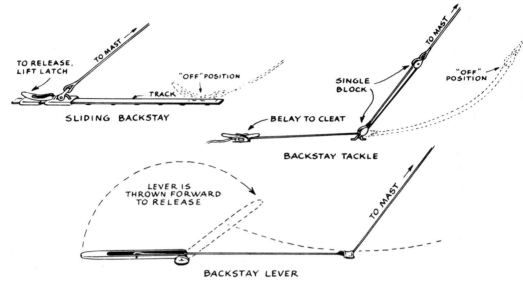

Fig. 100. Three types of adjustable backstays showing on and off positions.

2. Hull shapes, and the hard chine. The shape of a boat's hull is most easily seen by taking a cross-section look at it through the middle (Fig. 101).

Fig. 101. Hull shapes, showing differences between hard chine and round bottom boats.

The commonest small boat hull shapes have a *hard chine* — that is, a sharp angle where side and bottom meet. This chine acts somewhat like a keel when the boat heels, yet because of its curve on the leeward bow it helps push the boat up to windward while beating. A hard chine hull also permits a boat to have a wider and flatter bottom, which gives her more stability in sailing downwind.

The Snipe is the most common of the V-bottom boats, while the Comets, Stars, and Lightnings are typical of the similar arc-bottom boats. The International 14-foot Dinghy and its big sister the Thistle are lightweight round-bottom hulls and exceptionally fast. They are easy to plane because of the flattened after portion of the hull, and are sporty boats for the advanced sailor.

The fastest sailboats in the world, under certain conditions, are the Scows (Catamarans excepted). Their hulls are arc-bottomed, broad, and flat, without any sharp prow, and will skim over the water at great speeds.

3. The jib and new running rigging. Every sail has its own name, halyard, sheet, outhaul, and downhaul. So it is with the *jib*, our new small sail that hangs on a stay and has no boom.

Still, the forward edge of the sail is called the luff and the trailing edge the leach. But since the jib is attached to a stay rather than the mast, it may rightly be called a staysail (stays'l). On larger yachts there may be many staysails, usually named for the stays to which they attach.

Jib sheets. Unlike the mainsail, the jib has two sheets. One is rigged along the port side and the other to starboard, running between the mast and shrouds. On larger yachts with big jibs the sheets run outside the shrouds.

Jib sheets are rigged with a block and tackle arrangement to make trimming the jib easier, or else they lead directly through a block on deck, or a *fair lead*. A fair lead should be of generous size, with a wide flange that will help prevent pulling the sheet at sharp angles, which tends to break the fibers and weaken the line.

Only one sheet is used at a time. When beating, this is the sheet *to leeward*. The windward sheet is slack and not tightened until you come about on the other tack.

4. Theory of wind flow with jib and mainsail. Although the jib acts like any other sail with its own pocket, airfoil and wind currents, it has another effect — that of producing a "slot" (Fig. 102).

Wind that passes between jib and mainsail goes through an opening that gets more and more narrow, like a funnel. The effect of this is to make this air move faster. This in turn causes a low-pressure area on the back of the sail and allows the sail to be "pulled" along as if this were a vacuum.

It is the same manner in which wind passing over an airplane

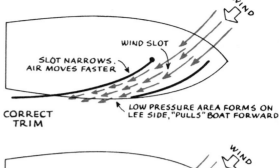

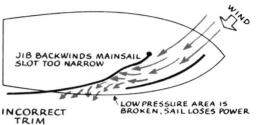

Fig. 102. The jib produces an air "slot" which narrows down and causes the wind passing through it to move faster, giving the mainsail more power.

wing causes a low-pressure area on the top of the wing. There is then a greater force pushing up from below, and the wing rises.

This slotting of air between the sails, and the resulting low-pressure area behind the mainsail, adds great power to the boat . . . and is one of the most important factors to be considered when sailing.

5. Setting sails on the sloop. Whether you are hoisting two sails on a sloop, or five sails on a schooner, the principle is the same: the aftermost sails (those most to the rear) go up first and stay up longest.

This means that you start in the stern and hoist sails as you move forward, while in lowering sails you start forward and move aft. Having the sails in the stern up longest, the boat will swing like a weather vane and stay headed into the wind. This is the whole reason for doing it this way.

Therefore, in the sloop *the main goes up first, and comes down last.* If you douse the mainsail before the jib, you are just asking for trouble sooner or later . . . and it is a sign of poor seamanship.

Bending on the jib. You can bend on the jib (fasten it to its proper fittings) either before or after you bend the main, provided you hoist them in proper order.

Start with the tack and shackle it to the deck fitting at the bow. This may be a jib downhaul on some boats. Now overhaul the sail along the luff, running it through your hands to take out the twists and clipping on the jib snaps as you go. This puts them on the stay in proper sequence.

Look aloft and clear the halyard. See that it is not wrapped around the headstay, and shackle it to the headboard of the sail. Jib sheets are fastened next, but before you do so, be sure to overhaul the sail along the foot from the tack to the clew. Lead sheets through their fair leads and put in a figure-8 knot.

6. Trimming the jib. The jib is first trimmed like any other sail, by letting it out until it luffs and then trimming so the luff just stops. Then it has to be trimmed to get a good slot effect (Fig. 102).

If the jib is drawn in too tightly, it will deflect the wind against the back side of the mainsail, causing the main to luff and break its airfoil shape, and you will lose power. To prevent this backwinding, the jib may be let out slightly. If this causes it to luff, the jib should be trimmed in again and the mainsail also trimmed in.

On some boats the mainsail will always carry a small luff in moderate or strong winds. This is most likely because the mainsail is very full (a deep pocket) and the wind strikes the lee side more easily. But if the mainsail is flat, the cause may be in the boat's design and can't be remedied short of actually moving the whole mast aft a few inches or more. This will widen the slot, but unless you have had experience in aerodynamics, don't try it.

Reaching. Here the slot becomes less effective, since it widens as the sails are let out and the funnel effect is decreased. Therefore, trim the jib according to its luff, like the mainsail.

Running. Here the jib is put out on the side opposite to the main, called *wing and wing,* and there is no slot effect. To keep it out a whisker pole is used, attaching to the mast and using the windward jib sheet, since the jib is set to windward. The sail is trimmed at about right angles to the wind, but should have a full curve to its shape.

7. Duties of crew in handling jib. Your crew is responsible for trimming the jib as outlined above.

Backwinding the jib. In getting away from docks and moorings, or in getting out of irons, it may help to pull on the windward jib sheet and backwind the jib. This causes the jib to fill from the lee side and will give you sternway much sooner.

Coming about. If your boat does not have adjustable backstays, the crew's duties in tacking are to handle the jib and shift his weight to the opposite side. Keeping the boat heeled at the proper angle for sailing is a job the crew should tend to constantly, sitting inboard or hiking out, as the case may be.

Sometimes crew can handle both main and jib sheets. However, in heavy weather crew will have all he can handle to bring the jib around and trim it in, so skipper should take the mainsheet. This requires no trimming and can probably be held with a round turn on a cleat or a slippery hitch while coming about.

How to handle jib in tacking. Skipper eases the tiller hard alee and lets the boat round up into the wind. Crew still keeps the jib sheet tight. Only when the jib "breaks" by showing a good-sized luff should he ease the leeward sheet. He then starts to shift his weight to the other side, and when he feels the jib go slack he begins to trim in rapidly on the new sheet.

Managing the backstays. When the boat is headed directly into the wind with both mainsail and jib luffing, the crew puts on the new backstay while the skipper lets off the old (Fig. 103). If both stays happen to be off or on at the same time, it will make no difference as long as the boat is headed into the wind. But the stays must be set correctly before you fill away again on the new tack.

Troubles to avoid. The commonest mistake in handling the jib is to let go of the old sheet too soon, losing that extra bit of driving power still in the sail as it starts to luff. This is sometimes followed by rapidly trimming the new sheet too soon, before the boat is around, causing the jib to backwind and slow the boat. Crew must keep a sharp eye on the sail and wait for the jib to really "break" before changing sheets.

At other times, the jib sheet that is let off will jam in its block, preventing the jib from coming across in front of the mast. A good crew should give the old sheet plenty of slack after he has let go and see that it is not tangled in the cockpit or on deck.

Avoid confusion with backstays. Crew may handle both, skip-

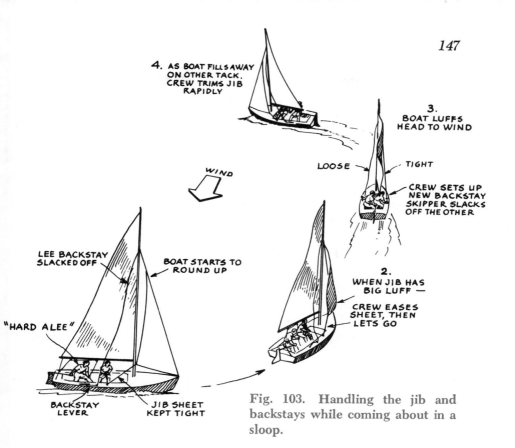

Fig. 103. Handling the jib and backstays while coming about in a sloop.

per may handle both, or you may each take one. The main thing is to know what each person is supposed to do when tacking . . . and then follow this same routine every time.

Occasionally a backstay will be missed and not be put on in time. If the sails start to fill, the jib will pull the mast forward at an alarming angle because there is nothing supporting the mast from astern. To correct this, head up at once until the sails luff, and put the windward stay on.

Setting the whisker pole the easy way. It is best if crew can set the whisker pole from the cockpit. Here his weight is kept lower, which gives the boat more stability on the run with less chance of tipping over.

It is often difficult to get hold of the jib to fasten the whisker pole, as the sail is usually flapping around somewhere out ahead of the boat. A way to do it easily is to hold pole and jib sheet together in one hand, then run the other out the pole, which brings the clew of the sail in near the tip of the pole (Fig. 104). Hook them together, then keep tension on the jib sheet and fit the other end of the pole to the mast.

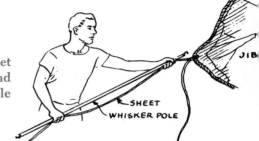

Fig. 104. Crew holds one jib sheet and pole together, then runs hand out along them to bring tip of pole and sail together quickly.

Jibing the sloop. The technique of jibing is the same as in the smaller catboat. But the sail is larger and there is more danger of doing damage if the jibe is accidental or not carried out properly. Again, the mainsail must be brought in by the sheet, then payed out hand over hand on the other side.

Crew can handle the jib and both backstays while skipper handles the tiller and mainsheet (Fig. 105).

To save time, crew should put the whisker pole into the cockpit on the leeward side, where it will be ready for use when the jibe is completed. However, the crew's most important job is to change the

Fig. 105. Technique of jibing the small sloop.

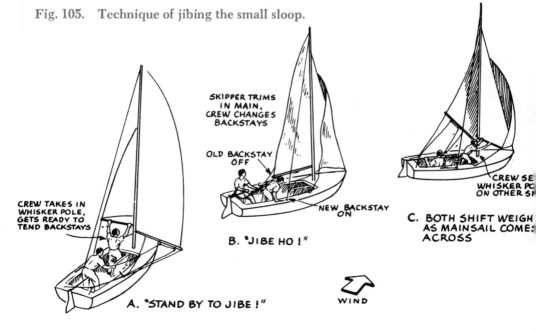

backstays, and while doing this he can forget the jib entirely. The new backstay can be put on as soon as the boom is in far enough to permit it. The old one is then let off, so that the mast is continually supported while the jibe is taking place. Be sure both backstays are never off at the same time during the jibe, as you may lose your rigging if the wind is strong enough!

8. Sailing the sloop in heavy weather. (Fig. 106). The first requirement to sailing the sloop when winds are strong is to have a properly setting jib. This means that the jibstay must be tight and the halyard tight. Most jibs have a wire rope in the luff (which is pulled tight by the halyard), and this must be just as taut as the jibstay. Otherwise the jib will sag to leeward and lose much of its effect.

WIND

MAINSAIL
LUFFING

JIB IS KEPT
FULL
WITH SHEET
TRIMMED
IN

SKIPPER
EASES UP INTO
WIND

Fig. 106. The steps in keeping the boat flat in heavy weather are: a. hike out, b. head up, and c. luff the mainsail.

Keep the jib sheet well trimmed. The main driving force of the boat depends on the jib, because of the important slot effect. For this reason the jib must be kept tightly trimmed and free of a luff. This is tough work for the crew . . . and is especially hard on the hands.

Don't wrap the sheet around your wrists, as this will simply cut off the circulation and make your hands ache. A better way is to double the sheet in your palm, with the loop going over your thumb. If you want, cut the fingers off an old leather or cloth glove and use it while handling sheets.

Sail the boat on an even keel. The sloop should be sailed as flat as possible, even when beating. The reason for this is partly that large waves form on the leeward side when heeling, and partly that less sail area is exposed to the wind. Both these reduce speed considerably.

Hike out first, then head up. The boat will do best if both sails are trimmed close-hauled in heavy weather, provided you can prevent heeling and can sail the boat flat. You and your crew must hike out to windward, using hiking straps and a tiller extension to help get your weight outboard.

If hiking does not keep you from heeling excessively, let the boat round up into the wind with each puff. In this way you will work up to windward at the same time you spill some wind from the sails.

Luff the mainsail, not the jib. If the wind is so strong or gusty that hiking out and rounding up are not enough to keep from heeling, the mainsail should be eased out. The jib will still have great driving power, even if the mainsail carries a large luff. Easing the main will also reduce weather helm, which you probably will have from the strong winds (see Chapter 11).

However, the jib must be kept trimmed tightly if you are to sail well with a luff in the main. Again, you'll need a strong crew with tough hands!

9. Sailing in light airs. The principles of slacking sheets slightly, shaping sails to increase the pocket, using large and baggy sails, and heeling slightly to leeward, etc., all apply to the sloop as they did to the catboat.

The difference is that the jib is particularly sensitive to light winds because of its small size. Heavy jib sheets or heavy metal shackles on the jib clew will curl the foot of the sail and spill what wind you do have. Take off the blocks and heavy lines, then fix up some lightweight sheets to tie on for the drifters.

When you are running downwind the light wind may not have enough force to billow the jib. Have crew take down the whisker pole and stow it. He can then sit low in the cockpit and hold the sail out by hand to catch the faint breezes.

10. How to get your boat planing. Planing is the technique of sailing a boat on a reach in such a way that she skims over the water like a hydroplane, at nearly double her usual speed. Your boat should have a relatively flat bottom and be fairly light in weight. International 14-foot Dinghies, 5-0-5's, and Thistles plane at the drop of a hat. Comets and Snipes will plane in stronger winds; so will Lightnings, and sometimes even Stars.

The first trick in planing is to get the boat perfectly level (flat), so the hull skims over the water rather than buries her chine into it. To do this you will need hiking straps and a heavy crew — or a tall one.

When strong puffs hit while you are on a reach, get your weight out to windward and slightly aft at once, to put the boat on an even keel. Pull the tiller toward you and fall off a few degrees rather suddenly. If you can't fall off or hold the boat flat because the wind is too strong, let the mainsail out until you can.

When this is done, give the sheet a hard pull to bring the sail in quickly, and hold it there. This should do it. The boat will spring to life, and you'll feel it skim over the water on its own bow wave, throwing spray far out to each side.

Once you are on the plane, you can head up to your former course, but you must trim the sail in farther than usual. The reason is that you have so increased the boat's speed that the apparent wind direction is now more ahead, and the sails are trimmed almost as if you were close reaching or beating! By playing both jib and mainsail, you should be able to stay on the plane as long as the wind lasts.

11. Sailing with a spinnaker. The spinnaker is a delicate sail that requires a good deal of finesse and sound teamwork to handle, especially when the wind gets a little stronger. It is not for beginners. However, you may have a chance to crew on a boat with one, and you should know something about its use.

How the spinnaker works. The spinnaker is a spherical sail which is supported by its three corners. It billows out and upward in front of the boat, lifting the bow and pulling the boat ahead.

The foot of the sail is controlled by its *sheet* and another controlling line, the *guy*. These are identical, except that the guy attaches at the corner where the spinnaker pole is also attached. When the pole is snapped to the opposite corner (on the other tack), the guy and sheet change names. A *topping lift* (line attached to mast and middle of pole) supports the weight of the pole, and is often made of rubber shock cord on small boats (Fig. 107).

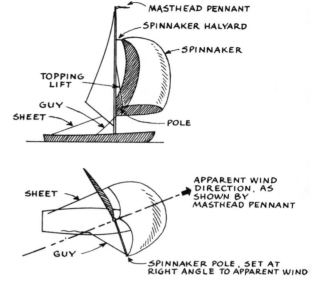

Fig. 107. Spinnaker set and flying on small boat. Notice that sheet trims far aft, while guy trims farther forward, and pole is kept at right angles to masthead pennant.

In trimming the spinnaker there are three basic points to remember. First, the sail should be allowed to pull forward and "lift" as much as possible, by slacking lines or raising the pole, or both. Secondly, the pole is trimmed aft by the guy until the pole is *at right angles to the apparent wind* (as shown by the masthead pennant), and is kept in this position.

Thirdly, the pole side of the spinnaker can be thought of as the *luff* of the sail, and the rest of the spinnaker trimmed accordingly. The sheet is let out until the luff of the sail begins to "curl." On a spinnaker the sail edge will curl rather than flutter, when the sail is luffing and about to collapse. When this happens, trim it in, but do it sharply with a good snap. This will undo the curl. Pay the sheet out again slowly to the point just before which it will luff. This is perfect trim.

Setting the spinnaker. The trick in setting a spinnaker is to make sure that *all* controlling lines — halyard, sheet, and guy — are outboard of the rigging and come to the folded spinnaker through the same fore triangle (Fig. 107A).

In the small-boat racing classes, the spinnaker is usually rigged before the race starts. It is stowed in a box or bag forward of the

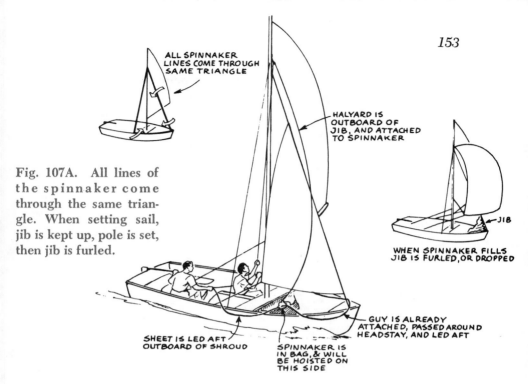

ALL SPINNAKER
LINES COME THROUGH
SAME TRIANGLE

HALYARD IS
OUTBOARD OF
JIB, AND ATTACHED
TO SPINNAKER

JIB

WHEN SPINNAKER FILLS
JIB IS FURLED, OR DROPPED

GUY IS ALREADY
ATTACHED, PASSED AROUND
HEADSTAY, AND LED AFT

SHEET IS LED AFT
OUTBOARD OF SHROUD

SPINNAKER IS
IN BAG, & WILL
BE HOISTED ON
THIS SIDE

Fig. 107A. All lines of the spinnaker come through the same triangle. When setting sail, jib is kept up, pole is set, then jib is furled.

mast on either side. Sheet and guy are attached and led outboard of shrouds and around the headstay, and halyard is snapped on (Fig. 107A). When ready to set the spinnaker, the bag is opened or the box put on deck, but the sail must be hoisted on the side on which it was rigged. It is then trimmed around the forestay after hoisting, depending on the wind direction. The pole is put on, snapped to the sail on the side *opposite* to the main boom. When the spinnaker fills, the jib is lowered or is furled up against the jibstay.

This method of hoisting the spinnaker on either the windward or leeward side is not suitable on boats where a larger spinnaker must be hoisted in the lee of the mainsail. However, it is an extremely fast method of hoisting and does away with having a man crawl forward during the race to pass the guy around the forestay.

Jibing. The spinnaker can be jibed without collapsing, so no time is lost on the downwind leg. If possible, all work should be done from the cockpit to give the boat more stability.

The procedure is simple. Detach the spinnaker pole from the mast and hook it onto the other clew, so the pole attaches to both corners at the foot. When the skipper jibes the mainsail, trip the line on the spinnaker pole, which will release the snap hook on the old corner, and snap this end of the pole to the mast (Fig. 108). In the meantime, another crew member trims the pole aft and lets out the new sheet, so the sail will lift and fill out on the new tack.

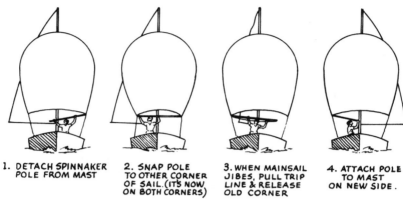

1. DETACH SPINNAKER POLE FROM MAST 2. SNAP POLE TO OTHER CORNER OF SAIL. (ITS NOW ON BOTH CORNERS) 3. WHEN MAINSAIL JIBES, PULL TRIP LINE & RELEASE OLD CORNER 4. ATTACH POLE TO MAST ON NEW SIDE.

Fig. 108. The proper steps in jibing with the spinnaker.

Dousing the spinnaker. If the wind is strong, getting the spinnaker in will require good teamwork and some know-how. Above all, don't let it get into the water; you may lose it.

Hoist the jib first, then let the spinnaker pole go forward until the spinnaker swings around into the lee of the mainsail and jib and is blanketed. If the pole is already forward and against the forestay (because you are on a broad reach), *fall off on a run* until the spinnaker is blanketed.

Once blanketed, the sail will collapse, and the pole can be unsnapped from the sail and mast. The foot of the spinnaker is hauled in by the man forward, working under the jib, while another crewman slowly lowers the halyard. If the sail is stuffed carefully into its bag or box, with all lines left attached, it will be ready to hoist next time you come around on the course.

EXERCISES

QUESTIONS

1. What is a fair lead?
2. On a sloop, why is the jib brought down first?
3. What is the usual reason the mainsail gets backwinded?
4. Name two ways you can correct backwind.
5. When does the crew let go the old jib sheet?
6. What is the advantage of having backstays on a sloop?

7. What is planing?
8. Name three things that you can do to help get your boat on a plane.
9. On the sloop pictured here (Fig. 109), write in names of all the parts that are numbered.

1. _____
2. _____
3. _____
4. _____
5. _____
6. _____
7. _____
8. _____
9. _____
10. _____
11. _____
12. _____
13. _____
14. _____
15. _____

Fig. 109.

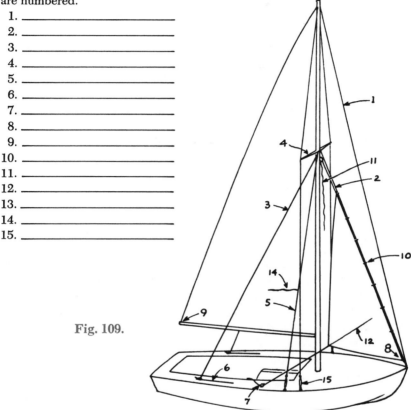

10. On the sloop pictured (Fig. 109), answer the following questions: Which sail is hoisted first? _____. Which is hoisted second? _____. Which sail is doused first? _____. Why?

11. Answer true or false:
   (a) _____ Jumper stays run from jumper strut to deck.
   (b) _____ There are adjustable backstays of some kind on all sloops.
   (c) _____ The halyard for the mainsail is always cleated on the starboard side.
   (d) _____ When a boat jibes, the "on" backstay must be let off.
   (e) _____ All round-bottom boats have a hard chine for easy planing.
   (f) _____ The trailing edge of the jib is closer to the mast, and so it is called the "luff."

(g) _____ The space between the jib and mainsail is called the "slot" because the wind funnels through it faster.

(h) _____ "Aftermost" means farthest to the rear.

(i) _____ The mainsail is always put up first and taken down first.

(j) _____ "Dousing the jib" means throwing it into the water after a race.

(k) _____ "Bending" a sail is a method of folding it for storage in a sea bag.

(l) _____ Some jibs have no downhaul.

(m)_____ Figure-8 knots are not used on jib sheets.

(n) _____ When coming about in a sloop, the jib has to be trimmed again, while the main does not.

(o) _____ On each tack, skipper and crew should take turns handling different backstays.

(p) _____ When luffing head to wind, it is dangerous to have both backstays off at the same time.

(q) _____ After tacking, backstay must be on before jib can be trimmed.

(r) _____ Crew should handle mainsail if jibing in a heavy wind.

(s) _____ In heavy winds it is more important to keep the main trimmed in tight than the jib, because it is the larger sail.

(t) _____ A slightly slack jibstay gives the jib a desirable curve to leeward.

(u) _____ Planing boats usually have fairly flat bottoms.

(v) _____ To get on a plane, boat must be sailed level (flat).

PRACTICE DRILL

1. Practice teamwork with your crew. Sail a series of short legs to a windward mark. Come about as frequently as possible on the way up, and jibe as often as you can on the way back. Try to do each job smoothly and quickly. Try different methods of handling backstays: skipper handle both, or crew handle both, or each take one.

2. In moderately strong winds, sail on a beat with both sails trimmed. Bring in the jib as far as it will come, and notice how it backwinds the mainsail. Bring the mainsail in farther. Does the backwinding stop? If the boat feels sluggish, ease the main a little until the boat gains speed. Now slack the jib until the backwinding stops or until the jib starts to luff. Somewhere in between is the proper set of the jib. Practice until you get the feel of it.

3. On a series of tacks, come about slowly, but let the leeward jib sheet out immediately. Now try a few tacks keeping the sheet trimmed until the jib "breaks." Notice the difference. When the sheet is cast off too soon the boat loses speed and loses driving power through the waves.

4. Practice backwinding the jib. The only way you will learn what a backwinded jib will do is to try it. Head your boat dead into the wind and get into irons. Pull either jib sheet tightly. This backwinds the jib and will give you sternway and soon push the bow around.

Next, tack frequently, but leave the old jib sheet trimmed in *too long*. Keep it tight while the jib luffs and even when the jib fills from the other side. Notice the effect of this backwinding. Sometimes this trick can be used to push the bow around if the seas are heavy and tacking is difficult.

11. Boat Care and Tuning

Tuning a boat refers to all the small adjustments you can make in stays, centerboard, mast, sheets, etc., to help you get the boat sailing at her fastest.

Many new young skippers feel that they have to have some magic bag full of tricks, or a special formula for moving the mast around, or the like, before they can tune their boats. The truth is much simpler, as any good racing skipper can tell you. The best tuning is simply good upkeep of your boat, and yourself.

1. General care of the boat. The hull is the place to start. If you keep it neat, clean, and dry — inside and out — you have gone a long way toward making your boat faster than any others in your fleet.

Keep the hull dry. When water is allowed to stand or accumulate in the cockpit of a wooden-hulled boat, the wood will absorb some of the water . . . whether the inside is painted or not. Over a summer sailing season this water in the wood may nearly double the hull weight, making your boat much slower.

Water standing in the cockpit also encourages marine growths and makes the cockpit slippery under foot.

Bail your boat out after each rain, and clean it out with a sponge after each time that you use it. If there is grease or oil inside, use some ordinary household detergent on it. Be sure all lines are coiled and that they are stowed up on floorboards or hung up. If left to soak in water in the cockpit, they will be stiff and hard to use and will soon rot.

Use a cockpit cover. Unless your boat is stored in a shed overnight, cover the cockpit with a large piece of canvas that will keep out most of the rain and dew.

The cover can fit over the boom and attach at the sides, preferably below the gunwales. It should allow an ample circulation of air fore and aft; otherwise the moisture inside will collect and heat up, promoting growth of fungus, mildew, and rust. A simple cover has both ends open to keep air moving through.

Open limber holes. In each rib of your boat, down near the keel or near the chine, there are small drain holes, called *limber holes.* These allow the water to drain to the lowest part of your bilge, where you can mop it up easily with a sponge. Limber holes plug up frequently and should be cleaned regularly with a small wire, such as the end of a coat hanger.

Be careful of metal boat pumps. When using a pump to take a large amount of water out of your boat, be careful that the metal feet on the pump are not chewing up the wood in your bilge. Set the feet on the floorboards, a spare bit of wood, or something rubber or metal. Better still, cover the feet with rubber bumpers, or get a different type of pump.

Keep small boat hauled out. Most of the small boat racing classes can be hauled out of water, except when actually in use, without harm to the hull. This will keep the hull lighter (less absorbed water) and will prevent the accumulation of marine moss and grass on the bottom. A small boat should be carried out of the water, or else rolled out on a trailer. *Never* drag a sailboat up on a sandy or rocky beach. This will scratch, chip, and mar the finish in short order. A wooden ramp that is equipped with a roller is satisfactory; otherwise the ramp is sure to have sand and grit on it which will scratch the boat's bottom.

Keep the hull smooth and clean. This cannot be emphasized enough. All the wetted surfaces — boat bottom, skeg, rudder, and centerboard — make friction with the water. This slows the boat. If these surfaces are allowed to accumulate marine growth, even a small amount, your boat will be even slower. The answer: scrub the bottom!

If you haul out, scrub the bottom once a week, using soap and sponge. If the hull is painted with a hard enamel, you may wish to polish it down once or twice a year with a very fine grade of wet sandpaper or with rottenstone. Rottenstone is a powder abrasive, is used on a soft cloth with water, and needs plenty of elbow grease.

If yours is a keel boat which cannot be hauled out conveniently, you will have to get underneath with a piece of scrubbing canvas or brush. One way to do this is to use a long-handled brush with a piece of cork or other flotation material tied underneath to give you pressure up against the hull.

Boats can also be tipped at a dock, or beached and turned at low tide on a soft or muddy shore, if there is no other way to work conveniently on the bottom.

Wash off salt spray. When your day's sailing is finished, wash the salt spray off your hull, rigging, spars, and sails with plenty of fresh water. The salt tends to dry, but when the air is moist it picks up the moisture and makes your lines or sails wet again. Wash down the hull with a hose. Small sails can be washed in a bathtub, or spread out on the lawn and hosed.

Be careful of electrolysis. This is an electrical action that occurs in salt water between two parts that are of different metals. The result is that one or both may be literally dissolved away. For this reason, you should not fasten any metal on your boat that will be in contact with salt water unless you know what the metal is and that other metal parts are of similar kind. If there is any doubt, take the problem to your local boatbuilder or marina.

2. Painting and varnishing. Most boats need to be painted once a year, some with hard racing enamel finishes need be done only every second year, and fiberglass hulls don't need to be painted at all.

Choice of paint. If your boat stays moored in the water, you will need an anti-fouling paint for the bottom and a good marine paint for the topsides and deck. Metals should be painted with anti-corrosive paint before all others. If you keep your boat hauled out and are interested in a hard and fast racing finish, enamels are the best. Marine enamel is good, but Duco Dulux household enamel will give an exceptionally hard surface. If you plan to spray paint, use automotive Dulux, as it will spray more easily and last longer.

Rules of painting. Here are a few basic do's and don'ts to re-member. Be sure all cleaning, sanding, and scraping is completed before you start painting. Never try to paint on a wet, greasy, or dirty surface. Don't paint on a rainy or damp day, nor at night out-side when the dew is falling. Paint frequently. Use thin coats, brushed in well. Clean brushes in paint thinner when through, then wash thoroughly with soap and water or detergent, and dry. Never leave brushes standing in a can of water or thinner, even overnight. Bristles will cake and crack.

Preparing the hull. If you are putting a new finish on your boat, the old paint must be scraped down to the wood. Don't use a paint remover, as this takes off too much paint. You want some paint to stay on in the grooves and grain of the wood.

After scraping, do any major repairs. You may want to round the edge of the chine, or streamline the shape of the skeg, centerboard, and rudder (see Chapter 8). Give the hull a sanding with medium-coarse paper and apply a priming coat. After this, fill any seams with a caulking compound or putty (use a hard-drying caulking or glazing compound if you plan to use enamel). Very small seams can be filled by working in some paint with a putty knife. Check for loose screws or plugs, and make these repairs. When caulking is thoroughly dry, begin sanding with finer grades of paper until you finish with a medium-fine wet sandpaper (such as #150 Tri-M-Ite). Wet sanding goes faster and the paper will not tend to clog as much as dry sanding.

Painting. When all filling and sanding is completed, wipe all dust off the hull and start painting. Brush paint in well, unless it is enamel. This must be "flowed on" in as few brush strokes as possible. Keep the surface to be painted level, not vertical, by moving or tipping the boat. Otherwise paint will sag and form curtains of thick streaks.

Allow paint to dry completely (about three weeks), then sand lightly with a very fine wet sandpaper (#220 Tri-M-Ite) and apply a second coat. For a new enamel finish, about four coats will be sufficient the first year, and perhaps one or two the second year. After that it may last three or four years, depending on the wear.

Varnish work. This is usually limited to the mast and boom, but may include the rudder and tiller. Varnish looks nice but does not wear well, and most of the "bright work" will have to be lightly sanded and revarnished twice a year or more. If varnish is left cracked and peeling, the wood beneath will become stained and dark and can only be cleaned by the difficult task of bleaching it.

The secret of good varnish work is the brush. Spend the money and get a good one, such as a badger-haired varnishing brush. Cheaper ones are too soft and will not spread the varnish properly.

3. Putting up for the winter. Many an old salt will tell you that the way to store a boat is near the water you sail on and in the same upright position as when sailing. This is good advice. Storage outdoors keeps the boat in the same dryness or dampness that exists in nature. If kept in a warm cellar or garage the hull will dry out and even crack from the dry winter heat.

However, the boat needs protection from the elements, especially ice and snow, so the ideal storage will be in an unheated outdoor shed. Otherwise a small frame should be built over the hull and covered with a waterproof tarpaulin. Air should be free to circulate underneath.

Keep the boat right side up. This can be done by supporting it along the length of the keel and at the chines. This spreads the weight evenly along the keel and ribs, as the designer intended. Putting the boat on its side or upside down across a couple of sawhorses will only encourage it to warp or settle in the wrong direction.

Remove all water from the boat, and take out the boat plug if you have one. Anchors, life jackets, bailers, and other gear should be removed and stored. Sheets, halyards, and other lines should be coiled neatly and hung or placed on a shelf in a dry, well-ventilated locker. Otherwise they will mildew and rot. Rudder and tiller should be stored vertically. The centerboard must be propped from below to take its weight off the boat, or removed entirely.

Mast and boom. It is very important when storing the mast and boom to make sure that they are lying straight. Look down the sail track, then support them in as many places as possible with small blocks to keep them straight. Don't just throw them up over a couple of rafters and expect they will be nice and straight when next season rolls around.

4. Tuning the mast. There are two general principles to follow here. First, keep the fittings on the mast as few and as lightweight as possible. Secondly, use the stays and shrouds to keep the mast straight while sailing.

The sailmaker designs his sails for a mast and boom that have no curves, and this is the way yours should be. On some larger rigs, such as Star, Atlantic, and International One Design sloops, the rigging is designed so the mast may be bowed. This is not advisable on smaller classes, unless you are an expert at it. However, some boats do better if the whole mast is tipped aft slightly. This tipping is called *raking*. We will see later when this may be necessary.

The best time to check the mast is while sailing on a beat. Give your crew the tiller and crawl forward and sight up the mast. See if it bends, then adjust the shrouds and stays so the mast is straight. On one tack the leeward shrouds will be slack while the windward ones are tight, but the mast will not bow or twist when changing tacks if the rig is tuned correctly.

Watch for broken wires. If you find these in your standing rigging, tape at once to prevent the sails from being torn. Then have the wire repaired as soon as possible, because one broken wire usually means others are about ready to let go.

5. How to set sails properly. One of the real arts of sailing is being able to set sails properly for any wind. How to adjust the mainsail in light and heavy weather was discussed in chapters 7 and 8. Now let's turn to the jib.

Setting the jib lead. The angle that the jib sheet makes with the jib is very important in determining the amount of curve the jib has in various parts, and therefore how well it works. On a new sail this angle of the sheet should aim just a little bit higher than the *miter* of the sail (the central seam), as shown in Figure 110.

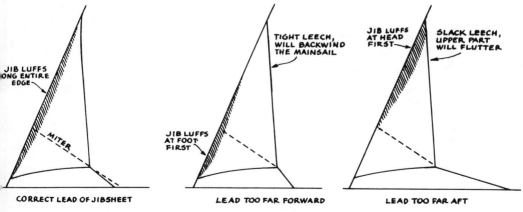

Fig. 110. The angle of the jib sheet runs a little higher than the miter on a new sail, and jib luffs along entire length. Incorrect lead causes sail to luff first near foot or near head.

Checking the jib lead. On older sails it may be harder to tell, or you may have bought a jib of slightly different size than before. When beating, jib should be set with a full curve along both leach and foot. As the sheet is slacked, or as the boat comes about, the jib should luff along the *entire length of its leading edge,* rather than first at the foot or first at the head (Fig. 110). This means that all of the sail is working effectively.

If the sail seems to luff improperly, move the sheet lead temporarily with your hand until you can determine the proper placement.

Mark jib sheets for beating. This simple trick will help crew trim the jib rapidly and correctly . . . and will make your tacking easier and faster. Sail on a beat in light weather and again in heavy weather. Get your jib in the best possible trim, then mark the spot on the sheet where it just comes through the fair lead or block.

Mark this spot with waterproof ink or sew in a piece of black thread. The heavy-weather mark will probably be two or three inches closer to the sail, since you trim in tighter for stronger winds. Now when you come about your crew can trim instantly to the mark, taking a turn around a cleat if necessary, before the jib has completely filled and is pulling strongly! Then he can make any fine adjustments needed when you are away on the next tack.

Repairing sails. Major tears should be sewn on a machine, and by a sailmaker (not an awning maker). Small temporary patches can be made with plastic tape, especially if the sails are synthetic. Check the areas of stress: batten pockets, bolt ropes, the head and tack, clew outhaul, etc. If there is undue wear on the bolt rope from a shackle or sail track, sew on a little piece of canvas to protect it. Inspect the slides frequently, and repair with waxed twine or button thread when necessary. A few stitches taken early on your sails will save you much expense and grief later on.

6. How to make and use a boom vang. When sailing on a broad reach or run, your boat would sail faster if only you could flatten the sail. However, with the boom out so far, the sheet pulls in rather than down, so a special device called a *boom vang* is used.

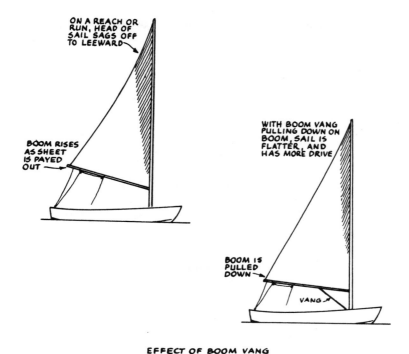

ON A REACH OR RUN, HEAD OF SAIL SAGS OFF TO LEEWARD

BOOM RISES AS SHEET IS PAYED OUT

WITH BOOM VANG PULLING DOWN ON BOOM, SAIL IS FLATTER, AND HAS MORE DRIVE

BOOM IS PULLED DOWN

VANG

EFFECT OF BOOM VANG

Fig. 111. On a reach or run the sail is given a better shape by using a boom vang to pull down on the boom.

The boom vang flattens the sail, which improves its aerodynamics and increases the boat's speed and efficiency (Fig. 111). The boom vang should be used by all sailors who race seriously.

To make a boom vang, follow these general principles. The vang has to go on and come off easily, preferably using large hooks or snaps that won't get tangled. The angle of pull of the boom vang is chiefly down, but it must also help to pull the boom a little bit out, not in, if possible.

Make some arrangement for jibing. The best way is to attach the vang to the boom and mast so it can swing over as you jibe. But this means that the boom must be up fairly high so the vang has a good angle of pull (Fig. 112). If the boom is low, you will have to attach it to something beside the mast, and this means it must be unsnapped before jibing.

Here are some methods of rigging a boom vang (Fig. 112).

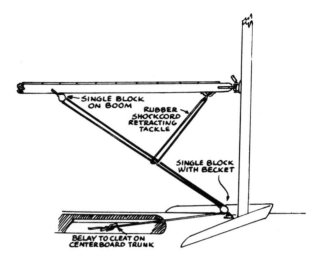

A. BOOM VANG WHERE BOOM
IS HIGH ABOVE DECK

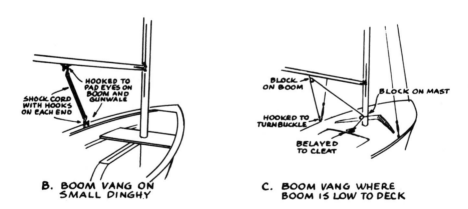

B. BOOM VANG ON
SMALL DINGHY

C. BOOM VANG WHERE
BOOM IS LOW TO DECK

Fig. 112. Three simple types of
boom vangs you can make.

7. Correcting improper helm. A boat has "helm" if it tends to head
up to windward or off to leeward by itself when the tiller is let go.

Weather helm. If the boat tends to round up into the wind, it is called weather helm. To keep the boat on a straight course it is necessary for you to pull the tiller up to windward in an effort to make the boat fall off (Fig. 113).

Lee helm. When the boat tends to fall off by itself, it has lee helm, and the tiller must be put over to leeward to counteract this and keep the boat on course (Fig. 113).

In both cases the rudder goes through the water at a wide angle — in extreme cases it may almost be sideways — and acts like a great drag, slowing the boat considerably.

Lee helm is dangerous. It makes your boat hard to head into the wind when a heavy puff or squall hits suddenly. Your boat will do better to have a small amount of weather helm.

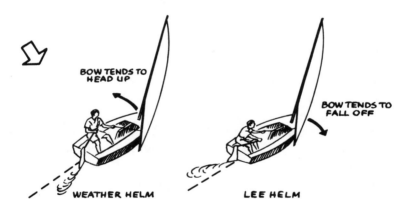

Fig. 113. With weather helm or lee helm, tiller must be held hard over to stay on course.

Factors causing improper helm. From a review of earlier chapters, we know that the boat turns about a pivot point located at the center of lateral resistance.

Wind pushing on all the sail forward of this point tends to turn the boat one way, and wind pushing on all the sail behind this point

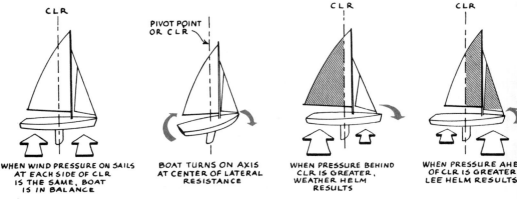

WHEN WIND PRESSURE ON SAILS
AT EACH SIDE OF CLR
IS THE SAME, BOAT
IS IN BALANCE

BOAT TURNS ON AXIS
AT CENTER OF LATERAL
RESISTANCE

WHEN PRESSURE BEHIND
CLR IS GREATER,
WEATHER HELM
RESULTS

WHEN PRESSURE AHEAD
OF CLR IS GREATER
LEE HELM RESULTS

Fig. 114. Forces of wind acting on sail area on each side of CLR tend to turn boat in one direction or the other.

tends to turn it the opposite way. If these two forces are equal, there is no helm (Fig. 114).

We can correct improper helm by changing any of these factors: the position of the center of lateral resistance, the amount of sail area on either side of it, or the effective force acting on the sail area.

Correcting helm by moving the centerboard. (Fig. 115). By shifting your centerboard you can effectively move your center of lateral resistance.

By slightly raising a pivoting board the main area is swung aft, shifting the area of lateral resistance with it, but the amount of centerboard in the water is reduced only slightly.

If your boat has weather helm, for instance, you can reduce it by shifting the center of resistance aft with a pivoting board. Or, if there is leeward helm, let your board down (and forward).

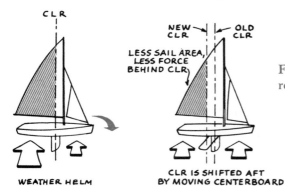

CLR

NEW
CLR

OLD
CLR

LESS SAIL AREA,
LESS FORCE
BEHIND CLR

Fig. 115. Weather helm is corrected by moving centerboard aft.

WEATHER HELM

CLR IS SHIFTED AFT
BY MOVING CENTERBOARD

Correcting helm by slacking sheets or by shifting weight. When you are out racing — especially in heavy weather — you may find that your boat has excessive weather helm (the most common), and you want to correct it at once. Two things can be tried.

First, slack the mainsail and sail chiefly on the jib. This reduces the force of wind pushing on the sail area behind the center of lateral resistance and will correct weather helm (Fig. 116).

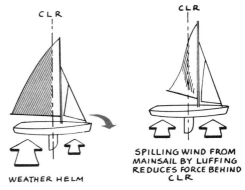

Fig. 116. Slacking the mainsheet causes some of the mainsail to luff, corrects the weather helm.

Secondly, shift the center of lateral resistance aft by moving your weight aft. This puts the stern deeper in the water where it offers more lateral resistance, and the whole center has been shifted much as it was when you moved your centerboard aft (Fig. 115).

Be careful not to shift your weight too drastically, especially if winds are light. The classic example is shown in Figure 117. Here the center of lateral resistance is so far to the stern that nearly all sail is forward of it and is pushing the boat off to leeward. No wonder the skipper can't get his boat to point!

Fig. 117.   Position of live ballast shifts CLR and affects balance, keeps small boat from pointing.

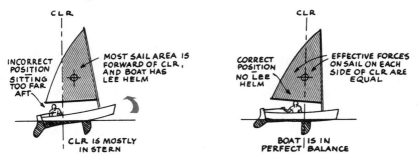

Fig. 118. Raking mast aft puts more sail area behind the CLR and corrects lee helm.

LEE HELM   MAST RAKED AFT

Correcting helm by changing rake of mast. Raking the mast shifts a lot of sail area forward and aft, so that this method of correcting helm must be used only as a last resort when other methods fail.

If your boat has a persistent lee helm, and the centerboard is as far forward as possible, try raking the mast aft. This shifts more sail area behind the center of lateral resistance and should correct it (**Fig. 118**). In most cases the mast should not be raked forward of the vertical.

SUMMARY OF HOW TO CORRECT IMPROPER HELM:

Correct by changing	For lee helm	For weather helm
(1) trim of sail	mainsail in, jib out	mainsail out, jib in
(2) weight	move forward	move aft
(3) centerboard	move forward	move aft
(4) mast rake	rake aft	reduce rake aft

8. Tuning yourself and your crew. Racing is a business that takes practice and teamwork. The top racing crews are those which sail together race after race, year after year. Skipper and crew know the exact duty each will perform for every maneuver in the boat. Not a second is wasted in coming about or jibing or trimming sails.

Get yourself a crew who will sail with you every race. Then go out and practice over and over again. Assign your crew specific jobs to do and then see that he does them. Rehearse jibing, tacking, rounding marks and other maneuvers as often as you can. The quicker you can do each of these things, the better your racing will become.

Don't forget yourself. Read all the books on racing and sailing you can find. Cram in every bit of knowledge you can get, and be ready with it on the day of the race.

EXERCISES

1. Increase your vocabulary. Define the following words:

(a) Electrolysis	(i) Rake
(b) Fiberglass	(j) Fair lead
(c) Tuning	(k) Weather helm
(d) Sheave	(l) Diamonds
(e) Chock	(m) Backwind
(f) Bilge	(n) Bending sail
(g) Limber hole	(o) Marconi rig
(h) Aloft	

2. Answer the following questions with short answers:
    (a) Why should salt spray be washed off boat and sails?
    (b) If the jib consistently backwinds the mainsail, could it be because the jib sheet lead is too far forward?
       How would you test it?
    (c) Which way does the boat tend to head if there is lee helm?
    (d) Name four ways you can try to correct weather helm.
    (e) As a racing skipper, how can you tune yourself?
3. Make a slow boat go faster. In the list below, circle the letter of each thing which will help make your boat go faster.
    (a) Keep boat dry, bail it out, use cockpit cover.
    (b) Grease sail track and backstay track with Vaselene.
    (c) Let bottom get slimy and slippery with marine growth and algae.
    (d) Keep shrouds tight so mast does not bend sideways.
    (e) Keep jibstay slack, to give nice leeward curve to jib.
    (f) Rub rottenstone on boat's bottom before sailing.
    (g) Keep fittings on the mast lightweight and as few as possible.
    (h) Remove excess coats of paint from deck and topsides.
    (i) Let mainsheet drag in water to get wet if wind is light.
    (j) If boat isn't pointing well, skipper and crew sit in stern.
    (k) Practice teamwork with crew in coming about and jibing.
    (l) If boat comes about too slowly, skipper and crew sit closer together.
    (m) Smooth the centerboard with steel wool or fine sandpaper.
4. Count the total number of things you have found in the list above which will make your boat go faster. If each one saves you 10 seconds, how much time did you gain in this race?_____. If every 9 seconds would let you beat an extra boat, how many more boats would you beat?_____.
5. Answer true or false:
    (a) _____ The best type of cockpit cover allows no water or wind to blow in anywhere.
    (b) _____ Even though bottom is smooth, there is still friction between boat and water.

(c) _____ Liquid paint removers are not recommended for boats.

(d) _____ Regulations for trailer hitches and lights are given by the State Department of Motor Vehicles.

(e) _____ A good place to store boat for the winter is upside down in a warm garage.

(f) _____ Cleaning bottom, keeping boat neat, and sanding centerboard are all examples of tuning the hull.

(g) _____ A forward bow in the mast helps shape the sail for heavy weather.

(h) _____ The purpose of shrouds is to keep the mast straight.

(i) _____ Diamond rigs are kept tight to prevent the mast from bending.

(j) _____ When jib has wide belly at the foot and luffs at the bottom first, jib lead should be moved forward.

(k) _____ A little lee helm is desirable.

(l) _____ A little windward helm is desirable.

(m) _____ A small tear in a sail should be repaired at once, even with plastic tape.

(n) _____ Slight weather helm will slow the boat, but might help her point higher.

(o) _____ Hauling boat out once a year is usually enough to keep the bottom clean.

PRACTICE DRILL

1. Inspect your boat for repairs. Next time that you are not out sailing, take a pencil and paper and go over your boat from stem to stern and make a list of repairs or changes to make for tuning. Keep this list and start doing these things as you can . . . even if it takes a season or two.

2. Sail a tune-up race. With another boat in your class, sail two races, both short ones. In between these try to tune your boat — adjust centerboard, move sheet block on traveler, tighten stays, go over the bottom, shape centerboard and rudder, etc. See if it makes a difference in the second race.

3. Hold an inspection day at least once a year. See if you can have your yacht club or fleet sponsor an inspection time to see whose boat is in best condition for the season. This should include paint, finish, varnish, rigging, and sails.

4. Make a boom vang. Follow the suggestions in this chapter, and learn about boom vangs from your fellow sailors.

5. Understand windward and leeward helm. To do this, set out on a nice day close-hauled on a beat. Move your weight far forward, then far aft. Hold the tiller loosely in your finger tips and see how shifting weight affects helm. Do the same by raising your centerboard and lowering it, then by strapping in the mainsail as hard as you can. When through, tune your boat so there is just a slight weather helm.

12. The Elements of Racing Tactics

As you begin your experience in sailboat racing, you soon realize that the winning boats have certain techniques and maneuvers which they use in race after race to put them out in front. These bits of strategy and maneuverings are racing tactics.

To the beginner, racing tactics often seem quite complicated. And well they might. Entire books have been written on the subject and more will be.

However, the basic fundamentals of racing tactics are simple. With a sound understanding of them you will develop good racing habits and will be well prepared to learn the more intricate details later on. Here are the tactics which will help you win races.

1. Get the most out of your boat. Few skippers ever get their boats racing as fast as the boats can go. Most sit back and say, "I've just got a slow boat." The only thing slow is the brain behind the tiller!

Tune your boat to perfection. There is always one more little thing that can be done to a boat to help her speed. Keep working for a glass-smooth bottom. Check the sails and the condition of the sheets. Throw out the bits of unwanted articles that seem to gather in the cockpit. Go over your check list of things to do, as outlined in the last chapter. Then tune up the skipper.

Sail hard every minute of your race. This basic principle is so important it ranks first. Don't forget it. No race is over until you have crossed the finish line. Until then, *anything can happen!* A dying wind can becalm the leaders . . . fresh wind may blow your way and send you speeding through the middle of the fleet . . . the boats ahead may sail for the wrong mark . . . or the fellow next to you may just relax enough so you can get the jump on him!

Don't stop racing until you've crossed the finish. Don't let down for an instant. Even when you are far behind, make it a point to sail hard and keep racing. Trim and retrim your sails. Think and talk about your tactics, rules, and what the other boats are doing. Watch for the boat ahead to make a mistake. If you race every minute, you will see the mistake and know how to take advantage of it.

Don't oversteer. In the excitement of trying to work up to windward on a beat there is a tendency to pump the tiller from side to side in a constant effort to head up into the wind. This oversteering is sometimes referred to as "sculling," and the total effect is to slow the boat.

Each time the rudder is turned at an angle to the water which is streaming by, it acts as a drag just as much as if you had placed a paddle crosswise to the flow of water. Whenever changing course or heading up to test the wind, *move the tiller slowly* and only a small amount.

Don't overtack. Every time you come about, your boat will lose some headway and speed until you are off and sailing on the new tack. This means you have lost precious seconds to other boats which haven't tacked . . . and this can amount to quite a distance by the time the weather leg of your race is done (Fig. 119). Tack when it is necessary, but only then.

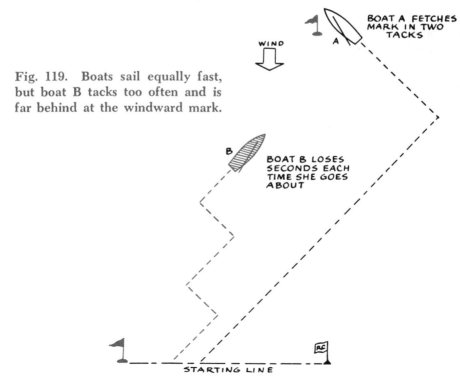

Fig. 119. Boats sail equally fast, but boat B tacks too often and is far behind at the windward mark.

Come about slowly. Because tacking is done so often during a race, it becomes one of the most important maneuvers for you to learn to do well. If you and another boat take the same number of tacks to get to the windward mark, the team which has done the best job of tacking will get there first. You and your crew should be this team. Work together until your tacking is smooth. Put the tiller over slowly and round up into the wind, letting the boat's headway carry her into the wind and around. The time it takes for you to shift weight to the other side, trim sheets, and hike out should be the same time you have allowed the boat to make the 90-degree change to the other tack. Shoving the tiller over fast or far only tends to slow the boat down, as we have discussed.

2. How other boats affect your wind. When another boat is within three mast lengths of you and is somewhat ahead or to windward, the wind is deflected by her sail and *will be less strong* by the time it reaches you. In addition, it may be coming from different directions, which also decreases its effective power.

The way in which the wind is deflected from other boats should be understood thoroughly, because it is a basic principle on which many racing tactics are built.

Backwind. When wind strikes the sail of a boat, it slides along the sail and then is deflected aft (Fig. 120). This deflected wind is called *backwind,* and will strike the sail of another boat on the lee-

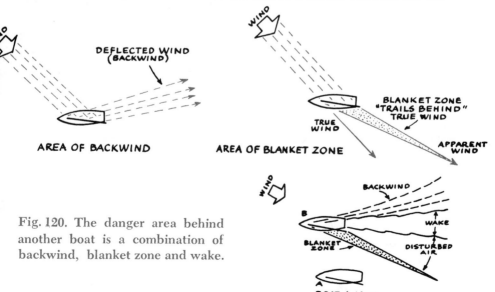

Fig. 120. The danger area behind another boat is a combination of backwind, blanket zone and wake.

ward side, causing the second boat to lose power and speed.

The most effective position for backwinding is to be slightly ahead and to *leeward* (Fig. 120). Here the wind bouncing off the sail will greatly affect the boats up to windward. The position is so good it is often called the *safe leeward position.*

If you are the boat being backwinded, the best defense is to tack at once to clear your wind. Every second that you stay in backwind means lost speed, since the backwind is affecting the lee side of your sails where the main driving force is.

Blanketing. This refers to stealing the wind of another boat that is down to leeward. On the lee side of each boat will be an area where the wind is lighter, simply because the sail has stopped much of it temporarily. This wind shadow, or blanket zone, extends out about three mast lengths (depending on the strength of the wind) and seems to trail the boat *in the direction of the apparent wind* (Fig. 120).

If you find yourself in a boat's blanket zone, you must get your wind clear right away, since the blanket zone contains nearly dead air with no driving power. Do this by changing tacks, or by falling off and getting into a safe leeward position (Fig. 120).

Most blanketing is done on the leeward legs, but here the position of the blanket zone is deceptive (Fig. 121). Even though you are directly upwind of another boat, you will not necessarily blanket her. This is because of the trailing effect of the blanket zone, which lies along the line of the *apparent* wind.

To blanket a competitor on a broad reach or beam reach, you will have to work well up to windward before the blanketing is effective. At the same time, you needn't fear being blanketed by a boat *directly astern* as long as you are reaching.

In addition to the effects of backwind and blanketing, a nearby boat also produces a fairly sizable stern wave and wake. This choppy water will also tend to slow you down, and should be avoided.

Make use of backwind, blanketing, and wake. Much of racing tactics is simply using these things to slow other boats down — by tacking so you are in a safe leeward position, or getting in front where you can slow another boat with your wake and backwind — or else avoiding them when behind other boats. Never stay in an-

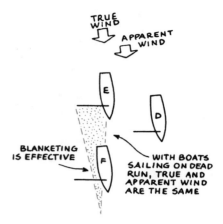

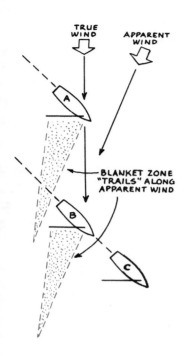

Fig. 121. The wind shadow of Boat A trails along the line of her apparent wind, so she does not blanket Boat B, directly to leeward. The same is true of Boat C. E and F are on a dead run, and blanketing is effective.

other boat's backwind, blanket zone, or wake any longer than you can help.

3. How to pass other boats. It will help if your boat is so tuned and sailed that she will point higher than your competitors. Even so, you must get by the areas of backwind and blanketing. There are a few tricks to help you do this.

Sailing through to leeward. By falling off and sailing through the tip of the blanket zone of the boat ahead, you can usually break through and gain a safe leeward position (Fig. 122).

If you are sailing close-hauled on a beat, this may mean that you will lose a little distance at first. However, by sailing hard, by pinching, and with a little luck, you can usually manage to pass to leeward and work up to a position where you are giving your competitor a good dose of backwind (Fig. 122).

On a reach it is somewhat easier to pass to leeward, because once you are through the blanket zone you can harden up on a faster sailing course (close reach), and gain a safe leeward position.

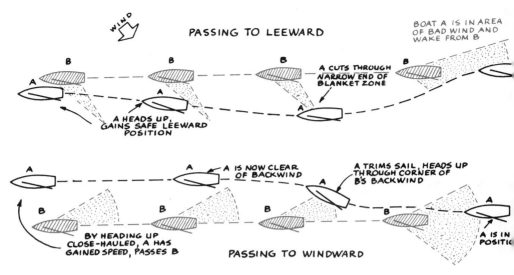

Fig. 122.   Boat A, in bad position, can pass to windward or to leeward.

In addition, on a reach or run, a definite advantage of passing to leeward is that *the windward boat cannot alter course and fall off* (to block your passing) once you are within three boat lengths. This is the rule (Appendix B).

Passing to windward. This is difficult to do unless your boat points higher and foots faster than the other boat. If so, going to windward is the best way to pass.

On a reach, breaking through to windward may be difficult because the boat to leeward has the right to luff you up into the wind. If she doesn't luff, trim your sheets and head up so that you sail rapidly through the area of backwind, not closer than one mast length from the boat ahead (Fig. 122).

Often you can pass to windward just by taking the other skipper by surprise. On a broad reach or run, surprise him just when he is setting his whisker pole or starting to jibe . . . or when he just isn't watching. One word of caution: *Be sure your centerboard is all the way down;* otherwise you will not be able to maneuver to windward!

If a slower boat tries to luff you to windward continually, so you cannot pass, try to get clear astern. Then wait for your chance — and pass her to leeward!

4. **Taking the windward mark.** Soon after the start of a race, boats will be spreading out on either port or starboard tack. Once your

wind is clear at the start, you must plan how you are going to reach the weather mark and which tack you will take.

Your objective is to get there as quickly as possible, and yet be there in such a position that you will have an advantage over other boats which are rounding.

Take the tack which heads closest to the mark. As you beat to windward it will become apparent that one tack or the other heads more nearly toward the next mark. You can find this out by sighting along your heading (the present tack), and then sighting at right angles to it (the opposite tack). One of these lines will point closer to the mark (Fig. 123).

By getting on this tack you have two advantages. If the wind shifts in your favor, you will not have wasted time sailing away from the mark. If it shifts against you (a header), you will not have to be in the poor slant so long. Secondly, it lets you get nearer to the mark, where it is easier to judge when to come about to fetch it.

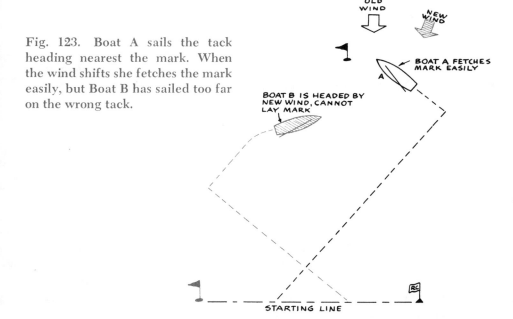

Fig. 123. Boat A sails the tack heading nearest the mark. When the wind shifts she fetches the mark easily, but Boat B has sailed too far on the wrong tack.

How to fetch the mark. By knowing that your tacks are at right angles to each other, you should be able to sight across the middle of your boat and tell exactly when you can lay the mark. Obviously, this is easier to do when you are close than when far away. Besides, when you are far out, a wind shift can cause you to sail much too far, as just mentioned (Fig. 123).

Most sailors can fetch a mark accurately from a distance of fifteen or twenty boat lengths and, with practice, even farther. But before you sail a course that will allow you to fetch it, you must plan whether you want to approach the mark on port or starboard tack. Many young sailors think that an approach on starboard tack is always the best, because this is the right-of-way tack. Such is not the case.

Avoid tacking at the mark. Knowing which side you must pass the mark on, approach so you can round without having to tack. This means that if you are passing marks to port, you will fetch the mark on a starboard tack (Fig. 124). You have right of way over other boats and can round without tacking, a good choice.

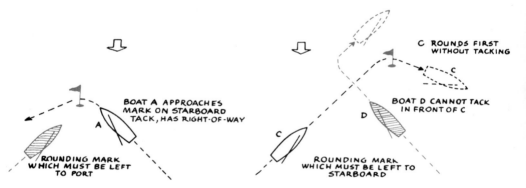

Fig. 124. Boat A approaches mark on starboard tack because she will pass it on port side. Boat C approaches mark on port tack, since she will take it to starboard. Boat D cannot tack at the mark and must let C go beneath her stern.

If marks are being passed to starboard, you should fetch the mark on a port tack. If you try to approach on starboard you will have to come about at the mark. If you are alone, this is fine. But if other boats are bearing down on the mark on port tack (Fig. 124), *you cannot tack directly in front of them* (tacking and jibing rule), even though they must keep clear of you. The boats on port tack will simply fall off a bit and go astern of the starboard tack boats, and on to round the mark first!

5. Rounding the leeward mark. The first rules to apply here are your basic principles of seamanship. As you approach the mark — but *before* you start to round — make sure your centerboard is lowered, your whisker pole is down, and that you have jibed so that you can round the mark without tacking. Now, what about the other boats?

Establish an overlap and get buoy room. Long before you get to the mark, plan to be on the inside of any other boats that may be near you. Try to gain an overlap so you can round nearest the buoy. By doing this you become the windward boat after you round, and you are in a good position to give the others backwind, blanketing, and wake (Fig. 125).

If alone, round properly. When approaching without other boats nearby, begin rounding before you reach the mark. Swing a little bit wide, then pass the mark while you are trimming sheets and hardening up for the next leg. In this way you will not sail any distance downwind that you don't need to (Fig. 125).

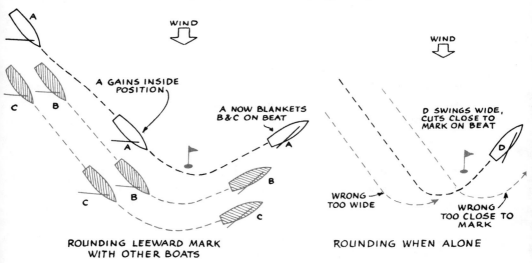

ROUNDING LEEWARD MARK
WITH OTHER BOATS

ROUNDING WHEN ALONE

Fig. 125. By gaining buoy room at leeward mark, Boat A becomes windward boat upon rounding, and soon blankets B and C. Boat D shows proper course when alone.

The commonest mistake is to sail directly for the mark, then turn just as you pass it. If you swing wide, you sail two or three boat lengths to leeward of the mark. If you cut too sharply, you lose all headway. The best way is to start your turn early.

Again, avoid tacking at the mark. If you must jibe before rounding, have this completed before the mark is near (usually two or three boat lengths). After rounding, stay on the same tack until you have full headway again. If there are boats behind you, wait and see what they are going to do before you tack. If they stay in your wake, you will give them plenty of poor wind; if they tack, so can you and still be well ahead.

6. What to do if behind. The most important thing to remember when behind is not to give up.

Watch the leaders. One good way to learn the lessons of racing and tactics is to watch the best skippers. If there are boats ahead of you at the windward mark, see how they got there and make a note of it so you can use the same tactics yourself.

During the race keep an eye on the lead boats. If they all seem to be sailing off to one side or the other, find out why. It may be because of a wind shift, or signs of fresh wind, or to play a favoring shore.

When in doubt, stay with the fleet. Sometimes the entire fleet seems to be sailing off in one direction or another without reason. Many a new skipper has decided that he will sail off in the opposite direction and outfox everybody. Don't do it unless you have very good reasons.

In the beginning, it is better to stay with the bunch and finish somewhere in the middle than to take a wild flier off to the side and lose to the whole fleet! By sailing with the fleet you are usually assured of being in the best wind (or at least the same wind as the others) and of being on the proper heading. However, you should take whatever short tacks are necessary to keep your wind clear, and not follow directly on someone's heels.

By following the expert skippers in your fleet you will soon learn their tactics, and chances are you won't do anything foolish which will lose you those boats already behind.

SUMMARY OF BASIC RACING TACTICS:

(1) Sail hard every minute of your race.

(2) Don't oversteer or overtack.

(3) Avoid backwind and blanketing zones.

(4) Keep out of another boat's wake.

(5) Gain the safe leeward position, and use it to backwind others.

(6) Take the tack which heads closest to the mark.

(7) Avoid tacking at the mark.

(8) Establish an overlap at marks, get buoy room.

(9) Watch the lead boats.

(10) Stay with the fleet.

EXERCISES

QUESTIONS

1. Increase your sailing vocabulary. Define the following terms:

   (a) Close aboard   (f) Backwind
   (b) Fetch   (g) Blanketing
   (c) Oversteer   (h) Apparent wind
   (d) Overtack   (i) Safe leeward position
   (e) Sculling   (j) Chop

2. Draw a boat diagram, as follows:

   (a) Draw a sailboat diagram, showing wind coming from directly abeam.
   (b) Draw the direction of the apparent wind, and show the blanket zone.
   (c) Place a second boat in the backwind area.
   (d) Place a third boat in the safe leeward position.

3. Give short answers to the following questions:

   (a) What is sculling?
       Is it helpful or harmful?_____. Why?
   (b) Should you watch mostly the boats ahead, or behind?_____.
       Why?
   (c) What is the one most important general tactic to remember in any
       race?
   (d) Why is it poor racing technique to put the tiller far over when com-
       ing about?
   (e) What advantage does the leeward boat have if another boat tries to
       pass to windward?
       Is this advantage more effective on a beat or a reach?

4. Answer true or false:

   (a)_____ Overtacking is helpful on the windward leg.
   (b)_____ New or fresh winds are generally stronger.

(c) _____ Sculling is a method of steering that makes the boat go faster.

(d) _____ On a beat, the port tack is at 45 degrees to the starboard tack.

(e) _____ Sometimes both tacks take you just as close to the windward mark.

(f) _____ If the wind shifts, the boat heading closest to the windward mark usually has the advantage.

(g) _____ If you are just a few boat lengths from the mark but are in another boat's backwind, it may be better tactics *not* to tack, and just follow the other boat around the mark.

(h) _____ A boat's stern wave and wake may slow down the boats behind a good deal.

(i) _____ Tacking in front of another boat to give him backwind is illegal.

(j) _____ Tacking in front of another boat is illegal if it makes him change course to avoid a collision.

(k) _____ Tacking at the mark is illegal.

(l) _____ Rounding the leeward mark as closely as possible is the best way to do it.

(m) _____ It is always best to take the windward mark on starboard tack, so you will have right of way.

(n) _____ It is good sailing to stay on the tack which heads you most directly to the next mark.

(o) _____ After you have cleared your wind at the start, it is useless to plot your course to the windward mark, because other boats will change your plans.

(p) _____ The boat rounding the leeward mark alone can do it best by rounding before reaching it, and passing the mark while hardening up for the next leg.

(q) _____ When the windward leg is half over, staying with the fleet is not such a good tactic.

(r) _____ Plans to get buoy room at the leeward mark should begin when you round the windward mark.

(s) _____ If it is crowded, jibing at the leeward mark is a good way to round it and make some room.

(t) _____ The most important thing to do when behind is not to give up.

PRACTICE DRILL

Learn the sailing principles in this chapter *by doing*, and putting them into practice.

1. Set up a small windward-leeward racing course. Find another boat which is just about equal to yours in all respects (just as fast, same class, etc.). With the other boat, do the following:
   (a) Sail around once, each taking the same number of tacks and sailing in the same general direction. This will show you how even the boats are.
   (b) Sail around with one boat taking just one or two long tacks, and the other tacking about every three or four boat lengths! When you reach the windward mark you will see how much this overtacking has slowed you down.
   (c) On the leeward leg, do the same thing. Have one boat jibe almost continually but follow in the same general course as the other boat.
   (d) Sail another windward leg with one boat sculling all the way, and the other not. Again, notice who arrives at the weather mark first. Remember, in light airs it is not considered sculling if you have to pump the tiller a few times to help the boat round the mark. Try it.
2. Try to sail directly behind a second boat while on a beat. Attempt to do it a little to leeward and a little to windward. After knowing what this does, sail with the other boat and get into a safe leeward position. From here try to pinch up and see if you can make use of your backwind.
3. Practice fetching windward marks. Choose a course marker or some kind of moored float. Approach it on a beat, and try fetching it from various distances: eight or ten boat lengths; then, twice this far; then try it from farther and farther away. Sail for the mark close-hauled each time. See how much easier it is to fetch the mark close aboard when the distance to it is not so great.

13. The Regatta

The high point of the sailing season is the regatta. This is when sailors from many fleets come to compete for various prizes . . . and to renew friendships of past years. Over a few seasons you will get to know the competitors from the other fleets well, and the regatta will be like old home week.

Usually many different classes of racing boats are competing, which lends much excitement to the event. For a night or two before the races you will see many new sleek hulls being brought in on trailers . . . you'll hear people singing and talking about races of other years . . . and you'll begin to feel the infectious carnival atmosphere which helps make the regatta fun.

Regattas are memorable affairs for the friends you'll make, the fun you'll have, and for the keen competition you'll get racing.

Types of regattas. In the usual kind of regatta sailors come from nearby towns and bring their own boats, racing for a traditional prize or one put up by the sponsoring yacht club. Sometimes the regatta is an elimination event for a particular racing class, where the top winners will be allowed to go on and compete in a national regatta.

Often it is impractical for sailors to transport their own boats, as when college groups or teams are competing from a long distance away. Here the host club may supply all the boats and let the teams draw lots for them. The boats are then switched in order after each race, so all sailors use all the boats. This is called a *round robin regatta,* and provides good competition without great expense.

1. Getting ready for a regatta. Suppose you are about to trail your boat over to a neighboring bay and sail in your first regatta. What kind of preparation should you make?

The most important work is done before you leave home. See that the hull is smooth and clean. Repair any parts of the boat that need fixing before you leave. Secure the boat on your towing trailer properly. Use crossbars over the top of the hull if you can, as these will hold the boat tighter and keep it from chafing.

Make a check list. It should contain all the items that will need packing: mast, boom, mainsheet, jib sheet, sails, rudder, tiller, life jackets, anchor and anchor line, paddle, bailers, ditty bag, tool box, etc. Give your trailer a check up, too. Put air in the tires, waterproof grease in the axles, and check the lights if you plan to drive at night. Your State Department of Motor Vehicles will tell you what the regulations are for boat trailers.

Clip weather maps from the newspaper. Learn to be a weather expert. Save the local weather maps for two or three days before a regatta, then compare them and see what the weather seems to be doing. With practice you can predict the winds and rain by seeing how the fronts are moving, and if a high or low pressure area is due to approach.

Find out about tides and currents. If you are going to race in strange waters where there may be currents, find out about them in advance. Local papers will usually publish the time the tide changes, and people living in the area can give you the best information on currents. Ask fishermen, marina operators, other sailors . . . anyone who will talk.

Arrive a day early. Unless you are an old hand at it, don't try to arrive for a regatta in the morning with the first race to start at noon. Much work has to be done, including assembling your boat, launching it, putting out a mooring, and registration. Many a sailor has hastily launched his boat for a race and discovered he has forgotten his tiller . . . or rudder . . . or sails!

2. Registration. This is an important beginning at the regatta, when you should get as much information about the races and course as possible. Register as soon as you can.

The race circular. This is the official sheet which will tell you the times the races start, where they will be held, what the starting signals are, and what the various flags mean that the race committee may fly. Get an extra copy of the circular and don't lose it. Go over it the night before the first race, and plan to take it with you on your boat.

Skippers' meeting. Before the races begin the race committee will have a meeting with all the skippers and crews. They will tell you where the starting line will be and how the races are to be run, and will give you the "official time." This is so you can set your own watch with theirs and know exactly when the races will begin. They will answer any questions you may have about the regatta.

3. The day of the first race. Weather is the most important thing to look for. Tune in an early morning weather report on your radio and write down the expected wind direction and velocities. Compare this with your own weather maps.

Take a practice sail early. Long before everyone else gets going, stow your gear aboard and set out on a tune-up sail. It will help you get the feel of the water, especially if you haven't sailed this area before, and will let you test your boat and rigging. You can get used to the wind, current, and landmarks . . . and have time to make any last minute repairs on the boat. It is surprising how many sailors fail to get out early enough to do this, for it is a good regatta tactic.

Take your race circular with you. If you can find a large-sized clear plastic envelope, use it to keep your circular in so it will remain dry. Some skippers even tape their folders down on the deck in the stern, especially if the race circular contains a chart of the area in which you are sailing. This keeps it right where you can see it at all times.

4. Start of the races. Tactics at the start are not much different in a regatta than in your own club races back home. The difference is that there are more boats . . . and usually a bit more confusion.

Keep clear of the restricted area. When there are other classes starting ahead of you, the area around the starting line is restricted to their use for the five minutes before their start. This area may be marked off with special buoys. Stay off the starting line and out of the area behind it.

Give way, even to port tack. Before your class starts there will be many boats milling around, making maneuvering difficult. Don't rely on safety just because you are on starboard tack. Keep an eye out and give way to anyone who needs it — port or starboard tack — until your preparatory signal is given. Then the rules of your race begin.

Check the course signals. As soon as the race committee boat has taken its station on the starting line, you should sail by and see what the course signals are for your race. These will be shown as numbers or letters or flag colors. Write them down. Then check the chart on your race circular and see where the race course goes. Always find out where the next mark of your course is, even if you need to use binoculars to find it.

Watch the classes ahead. One way to help find the weather mark is to see where the boats in the classes starting before you go. If you follow them carefully you will also learn whether those at the port or starboard end of the line got the better start. Use this in making your decisions.

Keep away from the pack at the start. Much of the fleet, especially if they are less experienced skippers, will probably try to start together in a bunch at one end of the line. If you get caught in this pack you are beset with wake, choppy water, backwind, and greatly disturbed air. Your chance of getting free is small, and you will soon be hopelessly behind.

To avoid these jams at the start, a seasoned race committee will spend much time setting the starting line, and will often favor the leeward or port end slightly. Your best bet is to pick a spot on the line where there are fewer boats, so your wind will be clear. This may be the middle, or way down to leeward.

Tack at once to clear your wind. This is doubly important in a regatta. You are competing against top skippers and there will be many who will delight in staying in front of you with their backwind and wake. But getting clear may not be easy. Often you are boxed in and cannot tack, or else have to work your way carefully through a horde of starboard tack boats while you are on port tack. This calls for good seamanship and careful judgment, as you don't want to foul out at the start.

5. How the races are scored. For regattas or for short racing series where there will probably be no more than three, five, or eight races, scores are given according to the number of boats beaten.

Each boat that crosses the finish line is given 1 point, plus 1 for each boat beaten, including any boats which were disqualified or did not finish.

In a twenty-boat race, a boat coming in second has beaten eighteen boats. He gets 18 points plus 1 point for finishing, a total of 19. First-place winners are often given an extra ¼ point, to prevent tie scores. In a twenty-boat race the first-place boat would get 20¼ points. Here is how part of the score sheet might look for a three-race regatta of twenty boats (Fig. 126).

Notice that the regatta winner did not win one race! However, his average was consistently high and this is what counted.

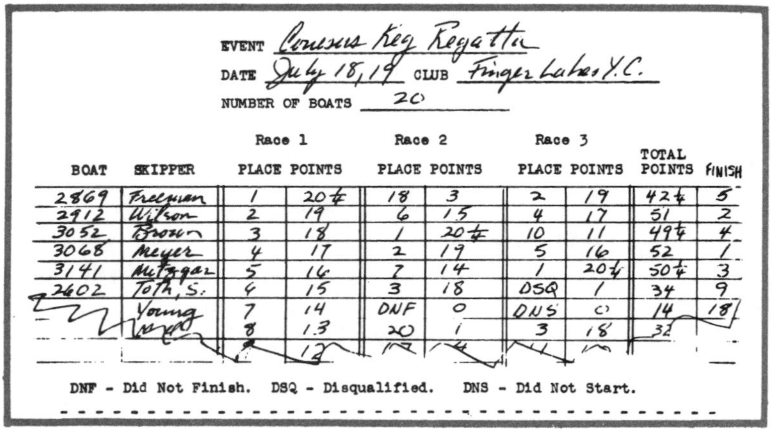

EVENT *Conesus Key Regatta*
DATE *July 18, 19* CLUB *Finger Lakes Y.C.*
NUMBER OF BOATS ___ 2O

BOAT	SKIPPER	Race 1 PLACE	POINTS	Race 2 PLACE	POINTS	Race 3 PLACE	POINTS	TOTAL POINTS	FINISH
2869	Frequen	1	20¼	18	3	2	19	42¼	5
2912	Wilson	2	19	6	15	4	17	51	2
3052	Brown	3	18	1	20¼	10	11	49¼	4
3068	Meyer	4	17	2	19	5	16	52	1
3141	Mutzgaz	5	16	7	14	1	20¼	50¼	3
2602	Toth, S.	6	15	3	18	DSQ	1	34	9
	Young	7	14	DNF	0	DNS	0	14	18
		8	13	20	1	3	18	32	

DNF - Did Not Finish.   DSQ - Disqualified.   DNS - Did Not Start.

Fig. 126. Typical score sheet.

6. Protesting a competitor. What happens when you are in a race and another boat fouls you? In most cases, if the foul was obvious, such as a port tack boat colliding with a starboard tack boat, the boat in error will drop out. Many times, however, both boats will claim they are right and the other boat wrong. The result is a *protest*.

In this case the race committee or a group appointed by them sits down and goes over your written request for a protest hearing. They will listen to both skippers, get out the rule book and model boats, and try to decide if the protest stands or not. If it does, the other boat is disqualified.

How to submit a protest. There are certain steps you must follow in order to protest.

(a) *Fly a protest flag.* When the incident happens, you must put up a small flag, of any color, attached to your rigging. Usually it is a small red flag which is clipped onto a lower shroud.

(b) *Report to the race committee at the finish.* You must display your protest flag as you cross the line, and then report to the race committee which boat you are protesting.

(c) *Submit the protest in writing.* Once ashore, write out the protest, listing the boats and what happened, and under what racing rule you are protesting. Then give it to the race committee.

(d) *Attend the protest hearing.* If the committee decides your protest was submitted properly, they will call a hearing, at which you should be present to tell your side of the story. If no foul was committed, the protest is thrown out and there is no disqualification or penalty.

Reasons for protesting. Many sailors have the mistaken idea that not protesting an obvious rule violation is good sportsmanship. Sometimes a truly fine skipper does commit a foul through sheer accident or momentary neglect, but this is the exception.

Most often it is the sailor who hasn't bothered to learn the rules, or who hasn't learned to sail by them. For a long time he has taken advantage of most sailors' natural inclinations to be easygoing and not protest. In any fleet he is a detriment, and in a regatta he is a hazard. You will do him a service to protest, and will help all the other boats in the regatta.

The rules were written to give order to the races and allow the best sailor to win. It is not fair that a top skipper be hampered or lose a race because a poor sailor failed to obey the rules and fouled him.

7. Sportsmanship and conduct at regattas. The host club sponsoring the regatta goes to great lengths to make it an enjoyable affair both on water and on shore. It is the duty of every visiting sailor and his guest to behave with decorum.

Good manners and sportsmanship are just as important ashore as on the water. Common sense will tell you not to litter the grounds with cut rope, lunch wrappers, beer cans or other trash . . . nor will you promote good feeling by driving your car and boat trailer over the yacht club's new lawn.

Lend a hand where you can. When it is time to haul boats out, take your turn at the dock or ramp and do your bit in helping the other fellows get their boats out.

EXERCISES

QUESTIONS

1. Write short answers to the following questions:
    (a) In a regatta, with more boats than usual at the starting line, what conditions would you expect to be different in wind and water?
    (b) What tactics should you use at the start to avoid these conditions?
    (c) What can you find out from watching the classes which start ahead of yours?
    (d) When other classes are starting, can you safely sail the area to windward of the starting line?_____. Should you?_____. Why?
    Can you sail in the area just to leeward of the starting line?_____. What is this area called?

2. Answer the following true or false:
    (a) _____ Regattas are for expert sailors only.
    (b) _____ At regattas you have to get out of the way of other boats if they are sailed by better skippers.
    (c) _____ All these things would be found in the race circular: time of races, starting signals, flags to be used, race results.
    (d) _____ It is not considered good sportsmanship at a regatta to inquire about tidal currents, wind variations, etc.
    (e) _____ Your check list for things to take to a regatta might include binoculars, first aid kit, tool box and protest flag.
    (f) _____ When the preparatory signal for your class is given, the racing rules go into effect as far as making protests is concerned.
    (g) _____ The race circular should be on the boat while racing.
    (h) _____ Taking a practice sail before the races start is a good regatta tactic.
    (i) _____ Racing in regattas is a good way to improve your tactics and sailing techniques.
    (j) _____ It's fair play to try and learn the "speed secrets" of other skippers whose boats go faster.

(k) _____ A protest should be submitted in writing and must list the rule violated.

(l) _____ Protests help all sailors know the rules better, and are sometimes made just to help clear up misunderstandings about the rules.

(m)_____ Reaching down a starting line is illegal at a regatta.

(n) _____ There is usually choppy water around the starting line, and this may slow your speed.

(o) _____ If in doubt at the start, stay with the majority of boats, since they will know which end is favored and you'll get a good start.

PRACTICE DRILL

1. Sail in as many regattas as possible. Sometimes this may mean giving up sailing in the home fleet series, but it will be worth it. The more outside competition you face, the better racing skipper you will become.

2. Make plans for a small regatta. Schedule a round robin tournament in your fleet, inviting competing sailors from nearby clubs for a day of races. Include as many details in your plan as possible, to get the idea of the vast amount of work that goes into the planning of such an event. These details include invitations, transportation directions, feeding, registration, preparing a race circular, finding a race committee and race committee chairman, getting boats ready, assigning boats, rotating boats, setting courses, scoring, awarding prizes, and final clean up and boat storage.

   Most of this work can be delegated to other people. Find volunteers in your sailing fleet, their parents, members of your club or sponsoring institution, etc. Assign as many jobs as possible . . . it will make your work easier and more fun.

3. Before sailing in a regatta, review the chapters on racing rules and tactics.

PART III

FOR THE
SPONSORING
SAILING GROUP
AND INSTRUCTORS

Part III of this book represents a deviation from the usual procedure in a book on sailing instruction.

Where Parts I and II have been written for the student of sailing — from the beginner to the intermediate sailor — Part III is written for the group that is organizing, sponsoring and teaching the sailing students.

It deals with methods of teaching sailing, how to organize and conduct classes, and what things to consider in the management and encouragement of a fleet of new sailors.

This section should fill a long-standing need for parents, civic leaders, small yacht clubs, and fraternal organizations which have wanted to sponsor and teach sailing to groups of youngsters and adults, but have not had the methods at hand.

14. Organizing a Program in Junior Sailing

The need to organize a sailing class is recognized anywhere by a few telltale signs. In your neighborhood it may simply be the presence of a large body of good water and the absence of a group of youngsters making use of it. Or it may be the sight of sailboats at their moorings or up on trailers throughout the weekends. Or a dwindling fleet of class boats with only a few die-hards showing up to race week after week.

These signs mean that young people have never learned sailing — or have lost interest.

Although many yacht clubs and camps have organized water activities and youth programs, too few make an effort to promote and teach sailing.

An initial spark to get started and some steady work will reward you with dividends. You'll see an enthusiastic fleet of young sailors grow before your eyes . . . and see the happy faces of boys and girls as they learn to master one of mankind's oldest skills. Here is how you can get started.

1. Sponsorship. It is not absolutely essential to have a sponsoring yacht club or other organized institution behind your sailing program, but it helps. Many classes have been started and carried through successfully by parents, sailing skippers, interested college students, and others. But the backing of an institution helps to guarantee the continuation of the program year after year and helps to provide sources of willing workers. Both are necessary.

Fraternal and civic groups are excellent places to find sponsors, and they do not have to be sea-minded and inclined toward sailing.

The Optimist Club of Clearwater, Florida, is a good example. For years they promoted such youth activities as the annual soapbox derby, but the hill in Clearwater is not very impressive and the expanse of good water for sailing is.

The switch was natural. Instruction was provided and their

young sailing fleet grew. A small 8-foot Pram was designed by the club, and boats were donated by local merchants. The program blossomed beyond anyone's imagination. Today, a dozen years later, the Optimist Pram is known throughout the world, and international regattas are held yearly . . . still restricted to boys and girls in the younger age groups.

Many small yacht clubs have watched their racing skippers come and go for years without benefit of sailing classes. Sometimes all they need is someone to start the ball rolling, make the suggestion, and watch the volunteers who will help with a youth sailing program.

If you find no sponsoring group, form your own! A group of interested Comet skippers in the Finger Lakes of New York started sailing classes in their own boats as a stimulus to building up their racing fleet. The idea caught on with the lakeside residents, and before long there were volunteers working on the race committee, in patrol boats, and at organization. Within a year the nucleus of a substantial sailing club was formed — and the racing fleet prospered.

Sponsoring groups are there, and you'll find them if you look.

2. Committee organization. Any sailing class or junior teaching program will need a behind-the-scenes committee of adults to handle details of management. It's a big job.

The chairman will be spark plug and co-ordinator, but such activities as class scheduling, procuring instructors, social activities, and publicity should be delegated jobs. In addition, you will need someone in charge of boat maintenance, but who can also instill in the minds of the fleet members the responsibility of taking care of the boats assigned to their use.

Another member will be in charge of the patrol boat, see that it is fully equipped at all times and that it is used to patrol the course and keep order in all races, and be ready to assist in case of accident.

As racing becomes more and more a part of your program, you will need a race committee and chairman. This should probably be an autonomous group which has charge of its own marks, guns, flags, boats, etc., and which will set up races in accordance with your season schedule. Work with them closely as to the number and length of races, especially when you want to keep the race course short for the beginners.

Larger organizations will have larger committees. At the San

Diego Yacht Club, the Junior Sailors have their own five-member board of supervisors, which works closely with the yacht club's senior board through a liaison member and the full-time director of youth activities.

3. Equipment and space requirements. You will need protected sailing water, boats, teaching space, storage space, some teaching aids, and people.

Sailboats. As shown earlier in this book, the best choice of a boat to learn in is the small catboat. Youngsters six to twelve years old can do with boats in the 8- to 10-foot class, while the thirteen- to seventeen-year-olds can handle 10- to 16-footers without difficulty. However, even adults get along well in the little 8- or 9-foot boats.

Price is most important. Keep it low and you will encourage interest. With the current big boom in dinghies, many boats can be bought in low-cost build-it-yourself kits. Kits are available in all prices, starting at $64 for a dinghy of rough-cut plywood, and up to $500 or more in fiberglass.

If your program is sponsored by a civic organization, it is usually easy to get a local merchant to donate a boat for use in the fleet, as the Optimist Club of Clearwater did. In return the merchant usually has his store name or insignia painted on the hull, much as sponsors of soapbox racers do.

Sometimes two institutions can combine use and expense. The University of Rochester shares a fleet of Beetle fiberglass dinghies with the Rochester Yacht Club on a winter-summer basis. The university students use the boats and facilities in the fall and winter when the yacht club classes are not in session.

If there is a racing fleet in your area, secondhand boats, discarded boats, and even rented boats in this class are probably available. Once the youngsters learn the ropes they will buy their own. This system was used successfully by the Ithaca Yacht Club on Cayuga Lake, in New York, and half the fun was rejuvenating the old boats that were gathered in for the new junior program.

In summary, boats should be small, inexpensive, single-sail, and seaworthy. If new ones are available, fiberglass is recommended.

Sailboat equipment. In the 10-foot class, boats should have a stubby paddle, bailer, sponge, bowline (painter), and a *life jacket for each passenger.* Life cushions are absolutely worthless in the event of a capsize and their use should be condemned. Bright-colored Coast Guard approved jackets are best.

Larger sailboats will need a small anchor, anchor line, bilge pump, and stern line as additional equipment.

The rescue boat. Before any sailing takes place, a rescue boat must be on hand. The only requirement is that you have one that is heavy enough and powerful enough to do well in heavy seas — as this is where you will have trouble, if any. Equipment, in addition to that already on board, should include extra life jackets, heavy towline, heavy storm anchor, lighter work anchor, anchor lines, fenders and boat hook. Inboard and outboard engines are both satisfactory, provided they start easily and do well in rough going.

Instructor's boat. A small boat for the sailing instructor will be of vast help in teaching classes from the water (see below). Any size will do, with outboard motor or oars, and a small anchor and life jacket.

Course markers, teaching aids, starting signals, and other equipment are discussed later.

Space for boats, in water and out. The area for sailing should be protected from storms and heavy seas, and should not cross a shipping lane or busy harbor channel. Dangerous shoals, races, and rip tides should be avoided. The area does not need to be large for juniors; as a matter of fact, a yacht club turning basin a few hundred yards across is sufficient. More space will be needed for larger class boats when racing.

Storage space. A building or shed to house the boats is ideal. In summer the boats may be stored outside, either ashore or else moored out if these facilities are available. The storage area needs to be adjacent to the water, and if the shore is rocky a launching ramp is advisable. A small dock with water deep enough for the boats on all sides will serve as a landing dock, and may even be the center of activity for your sailing instructor.

Teaching space. Some area set aside and designated for the sole use of the sailing class is essential. This may be no more than a shed outdoors on the dock, where the instructor hangs his hat and the students keep their notebooks. This is of poor service in rainy weather, however. Indoor space, such as a converted boat locker or the loft of an old boathouse, is better. Benches lining each wall can accommodate twenty or thirty students, and with the help of shelves and hooks, most of your sailing gear can be stored here, as well. A cupboard should be provided to keep teaching records and visual aids.

4. Instructors. The ideal sailing instructor is a scarce commodity. He should be a teacher first, and a sailor second. His character should be of the highest standing and his tolerance and patience unlimited. Since most instructors come from the ranks of sailors, it is necessary to instruct them in the art of teaching and equip them with the knowledge of time-proven teaching methods.

Where to find sailing instructors. If your program is limited to the summer sailing season, you will find many capable young men and women from the ranks of college students. The year-round program will need an employed instructor or youth counselor. Often these are found in retired businessmen, former scout leaders, teachers, or semi-retired and self-employed persons.

Volunteers and junior assistants. Once a capable head instructor is found, any number of other volunteers can be commandeered from the ranks of sailors and parents. High school students and young sailors in the racing fleets can serve admirably as assistants . . . but all should have some instruction in teaching. Before every class and lesson there should be a briefing session of instructors to cover not only the day's material, but *how it should best be taught.*

Student teachers. In each class the group can be more or less divided into those with some experience in sailing and those with very little. Pair them off, and make one student the teacher of the other . . . he, too, will learn by teaching.

5. Stressing dockyard and boat safety. As is obvious to all sailors, water-front safety is necessary at all times. Where children are involved, it is mandatory. The basic concepts of water and boat safety as taught to students are shown in Chapter 5 and should be reviewed by instructors.

Waiver of responsibility. Although serious accidents are extremely rare in well-run youth programs, it is best that the sponsoring organization require a waiver of responsibility signed by the students' parents. Actually, the hazards are about the same as in life anywhere, if proper safety precautions are taken.

Swimming requirement. All students must be able to swim, and some measure of ability should be decided upon, such as 50 yards, or 100 yards, and an ability to tread water indefinitely. There is no greater cause for fear on the water than an inability to swim well.

Instructors should be familiar and experienced with mouth-to-mouth resuscitation and know the procedures for rescuing swimmers and towing swamped boats.

6. Building interest in junior sailing. The clue to maintaining interest in the sailing program is to make certain that there is adequate recognition for the work done. This applies to the instructor staff as well as the students.

A progressive grading system is used in most clubs, where the students attain certain sailing ranks according to their abilities and the number of years they have been in the program. Awards of "Seaman," "Mate," and "Skipper" are given to students at the Pequot Yacht Club in Connecticut. Some will add a further award of "Racing Skipper" for advanced sailors. The term "Sailing Skipper" is awarded to the beginner who has advanced enough to captain his own boat at the Rochester Yacht Club and at the Onondaga Yacht Club in central New York.

Trophies, by all means. No matter how small, the trophy will mean a lot to the youngster who gets it. For years one club successfully used small wooden souvenir mugs costing about 25 cents apiece, by simply painting "1st," "2nd," or "3rd" on them.

There should be trophies for all your racing series, and others such as Bottoms-up Trophy, Most Improved Skipper Trophy, Best Care of Boat Trophy, etc.

A diploma or certificate should be given to each boy and girl who completes a season in the sailing course successfully.

Graduation day. Awards and diplomas are best given at a banquet or other festivity, often combined with some other yacht club affair. Its purpose is not only to award the students, but to promote good feelings with the parents and to give some recognition to the instruction staff and committee as well.

An elaborate graduation day program might include an exhibition boat drill and races in front of the spectators, followed by an awards luncheon. There are many ways to do this.

Publicity. The sailing program needs and should get publicity. Local newspapers are the biggest help, and if you can get to know the yachting editor, sports editor, or social editor, it will help. Newspapers want news, and sometimes you have to make it. Announcement of a new class or program meeting is worth while, especially if presented with photographs of some of the principals.

During the season, racing results should be sent in promptly by phone as soon as they are tabulated. Other publicity during the season will depend on how ingenious you are. A special sailing outing for the class, a regatta, election of new class officers, and the final banquet with awards are all newsworthy.

By keeping up your publicity, you will keep up the interest of sponsors and workers and guarantee a continual input of applicants for the classes.

Social activities. The ultimate purpose of a sailing program is to build character in young people through healthful recreation under proper supervision. As the boys and girls get older, the program must rightfully contain some social activities . . . but not on such a schedule as to overwhelm the sailing sessions or students.

Mike Maijgren, long-time chairman of junior sailing at the Rochester Yacht Club, solved the problem neatly by having some of the best social activities in the off season. A winter banquet and dance for students and friends kept spirits high during the long months when junior sailing was inactive. A family night, dockside fishing contest, and father-and-son (or daughter) sailboat race are activities you can hold during the season.

7. Adult sailing classes. Instruction should not be limited to the youngsters under seventeen years. Often there is a good response to the announcement of adult classes, which can be held in off-work hours (6:00-8:00 P.M., 5:00-7:30 P.M.) or on weekends.

Teaching principles are exactly the same, with the same emphasis on water safety, boat care, seamanship, etc., as with the young people. The difference usually is that the class is more orderly and easier to teach. Many a yachtsman will thank you for making sailing lessons available for his wife, because somehow she just never understood things when he was doing the teaching!

15. How to Teach Sailing.

Teaching is an art unto itself and teaching of sailing is no exception. The good sailor is not necessarily a good teacher unless he has had experience at it. But he can be good if he uses certain basic teaching methods, and makes certain adaptations to a classroom which covers a wide expanse of windy water.

1. Waterfront safety. Since there is a certain amount of potential danger in just being on the water, the first precept to teach in sailing is safety.

Keep strict discipline. The sailing class should be kept under control at all times. The best way to do this is to make sure everyone has something to do. If your class is large and must rotate through a smaller number of boats, be certain the remainder of students are *supervised* and are working on knots or engaged in boat repairs or some other activity. Trouble always comes when some students are idle or alone.

Strict water-front rules should include no running, no horseplay, and no scuffling. Rubber-soled shoes must be worn. Students should not be allowed to wander off the class premises, especially at dockside, and never onto moored yachts that are not for their use. Obedience to the instructor's demands is obligatory, and failure to obey is just cause for expulsion.

Safety in the boats. A demonstration of capsizing should be done early in the course to impress on students the fact that the boats do not sink, will support many people in the water, and should never be deserted before help arrives. A proper routine should be established for capsizing. At the sound of the instructor's emergency whistle, all other boats should immediately return to the dock — not to the capsized boat, where they will be a hazard to the rescue operation. Crews in the water should don life jackets and follow the procedure outlined in Chapter 5, and await the rescue boat. In the meantime, the other boats are safe ashore.

Keep boats together. When on the water, a single-file method of keeping the boats together is recommended. Each boat follows the next, according to lowest numbers on the sail . . . and all are under strict orders not to leave the group.

Wear life jackets. These should be worn whenever there is any chance of high winds, excessive chop, bad currents, or other factors which might cause boats to capsize. Many of us have had our only real scares when students tipped over, the waves and water were rougher than expected, and life jackets were not being worn. Don't put up with any student talk against wearing jackets; this is not being "chicken," just sensible.

2. Class lectures and curriculum. Through a three-month summer sailing season the average class will meet once or twice each weekend. Others will meet two or three times during the week, or perhaps on half days during the week. All will depend on how much of a crew of instructors is available.

Adult classes can be conveniently held during the hours of 6:00 P.M. to 8:00 P.M., while daylight saving time is in effect. The wind is often light at this time, but you may catch a steady evening offshore breeze.

If you meet in these early evening hours, it is advisable to switch the order of things and get into the boats right away for drills while sun and wind last. Lectures can come later with the dusk.

Plan the curriculum. An outline of lessons should be made for all of the sailing season. The chapter topics in Parts I and II of this book are designed as lesson subjects, and each chapter can be covered in one or two normal class sessions. It is wise to leave some days free, as kind of a buffer for stormy weather, and then to have special emergency programs ready in case the rains set in for a steady spell and sailing in your boats is out of the question.

Begin racing early. The basic sailing curriculum for beginners starts with fundamentals: seamanship, what makes a sailboat go, sailing to windward, sailing to leeward, and water safety. After this brief encounter with the boat, the student is ready to test his skills. Racing will do this. It should be worked into the curriculum as soon as students can get the boats safely around a short course, and they do not need to know the rules. Racing will bring out the natural feelings of competition and the desire to excel. It is the one best way of stimulating your class to sail better, and they will pick up the rules sooner than you think.

Divide and conquer. The sailing class should be divided according to its sailing ability and previous experience. This breaks down roughly into three groups: beginners, who have had no experience at all; intermediates, who know some of the ropes but who are technically not yet good sailors; and advanced students, who are usually older and are interested primarily in racing. This latter group should be kept separate from the first two, but they can be used as junior instructors.

Beginners and intermediate sailors work well together, especially when using the buddy system of teaching, where the more experienced lad will instruct the other.

When the class is large and the number of instructors or boats is few, dividing them into smaller groups is done just to be able to control them. Don't underestimate this. Plant a volunteer with each group and give a long assignment until the group can rotate through the boat work under your supervision. Small groups work best in all cases.

3. **Lectures should explain, show, and summarize.** The attention time for young people in a dry lecture is about thirty minutes. Don't make the day's lecture longer. Explain some basic principle, then demonstrate it with model boats or with a small boat out on the dock. After this summarize it, then give the students specific directions for doing it in their own boats, and take to the water. Lecture is over.

Notebooks should be kept by both student and instructor. While the boat work is progressing, make notes on all students. After each boat session there should be another short lecture. All mistakes and good points of the work are brought out — if possible, by the students themselves. The day's lesson is again summarized, and the next day's work assigned. This sequence of events teaches the student by explaining, doing, and summarizing.

Outside assignments can be given in books on sailing or racing, such as this one. However, the amount of work done by the student will depend mostly on his motivation. Here are some ways to help motivate him to learn.

Oral and written examinations. The chief purpose of examinations is to stimulate learning by recall, and to put a little anxiety upon the student to do this. A good system is to start each session with a short oral quiz, going down the line of students and asking different questions about the previous day's work. Some sort of grade should be put down in your book to keep track of those students who will require more instruction.

Where possible, have the student *show* the answer with a model boat and fan, or with two boats, or blackboard, etc. This reinforces the learning process. Written examinations are used in much the same way and should always be designed to make a point or demonstrate a principle. The series of examinations in this book are all designed in this fashion. Answers are given in Appendix A. If these quizzes are for grading or advancement, simply read the questions so the students will not be able to look up the answers at the same time.

Visual aids. Teaching is much easier if all the visual devices you can think of are used to make your points. The most basic of these is the blackboard. However, few people realize how much better the blackboard works when colored chalk is used. Try some. It makes the drawings more understandable.

Model boats of various kinds are excellent teaching aids. To demonstrate basic sailing get a fairly large one, remove the keel so it will sit upright on a table, and sew on a lightweight cotton or nylon sail that will move easily in light winds. The sail, boom, and sheet must all be workable. Place a large electric fan in front of this and you have as clear a picture of wind and boat as anyone could wish.

When racing rules are being discussed, small model boats of different colors will help. Remove the keels, but add to each boat a small screw on the bottom in the middle, so it projects down about ¼ inch. This will cause the model to heel slightly and shift its sail to one tack or the other. Course markers can be made from corks and matches, and a wind arrow from tin or wood. Keep this gear in a box away from the more playful students, or it won't last.

Help guest lecturers teach. From time to time you will probably have an old salt or a hot racing skipper come in and give a few lectures to your class. This is a nice change of pace, if the lecture is good, and you should make sure it is. Each guest should be briefed thoroughly on what is expected of him: that the lecture is to be short, that students are to be quizzed and are to participate, and that demonstrations are expected. Demonstrations may include anything from boat equipment, models, movies, or slides, to just a good chalk talk on the blackboard. In this way student interest — and learning — will stay at a peak.

A sample day's program. The rough outline for a day with a sailing class might look something like this:

8:10 A.M. — briefing session with junior instructors on day's work in jibing
8:30 A.M. — roll call
— oral quiz on review work: wind direction indicators, leeward sailing
— model boat and fan demonstration of how to jibe
— blackboard summary of steps in jibing
9:15 A.M. — class into boats for jibing drill, use windward-leeward course
11:15 A.M. — secure boats
11:45 A.M. — lunch at club, summary of morning's work and review of errors
12:30 P.M. — knot-tying review
1:00 P.M. — summary of jibing, summary of plans for race around practice area
1:10 P.M. — class into boats for short jibing drill
1:30 P.M. — three quick windward-leeward races, or more
2:30 P.M. — secure boats
— clean up and secure boat locker
— credit today's best skipper, assign lesson for tomorrow
3:00 P.M. — class dismissed

4. Methods of handling boat work. Ideally, an instructor should get into each boat and watch the student put her through the paces. This is impossible to do in a class, but as an instructor you can come pretty close.

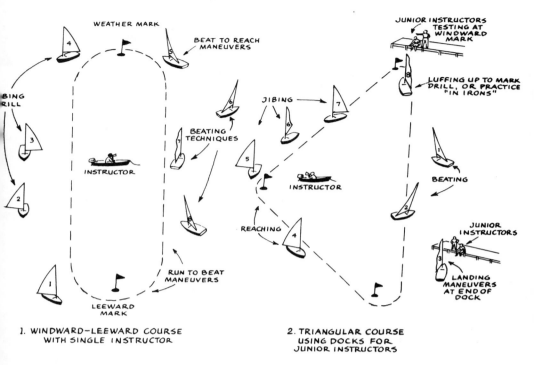

WEATHER MARK

BEAT TO REACH
MANEUVERS

JUNIOR INSTRUCTORS
TESTING AT
WINDWARD
MARK

LUFFING UP TO MARK
DRILL, OR PRACTICE
"IN IRONS"

JIBING

BEATING
TECHNIQUES

INSTRUCTOR

INSTRUCTOR

BEATING

JUNIOR
INSTRUCTORS

REACHING

LANDING
MANEUVERS
AT END OF
DOCK

RUN TO BEAT
MANEUVERS

LEEWARD
MARK

1. WINDWARD–LEEWARD COURSE
WITH SINGLE INSTRUCTOR

2. TRIANGULAR COURSE
USING DOCKS FOR
JUNIOR INSTRUCTORS

Fig. 127. Course markers are used to designate sailing directions and seamanship problems for class of beginners, and to restrict the sailing area.

The secret is to get out on the water yourself in an observation boat, and to keep the maneuvering area for the class boats as small and compact as possible. To do this a set of race-course markers is used and boats are instructed to go around them single file, in order (Fig. 127).

By anchoring in the middle of a small triangular course, you can observe the boats carefully and can instruct each one on seamanship by talking through a small megaphone. Junior instructors may also be set up at key points to take notes and to help instruct. Variations on this method are shown, to illustrate how many basic maneuvers can be practiced in a restricted area with a minimum number of instructors (Fig. 127).

Good discipline is necessary, as boats must be kept on the course and in proper order. The problem of slowing a boat down is also a good experience in seamanship.

The instructor will need a small megaphone, a coach's whistle, notebook and pen, and a strong pair of lungs.

The problem patient. Sometimes a youngster will just not get the right idea, no matter how many times or how hard you explain it. Here a junior instructor, or even the chief, should get into the boat and demonstrate the procedure with the balky student. A small transfusion like this, here and there, will often turn the tide in a student's learning of sailing.

Races for beginners. Initially, racing can be very informal until the basic rules are studied. However, it is best if races are started according to accepted tradition. Use your whistle, megaphone, and wrist watch . . . and set up a starting line between your instruction boat and the leeward mark of your instruction course.

If boats are small, a two-minute, one-minute, and start signal can be given. Counting out the last minute or last ten seconds is good teaching, and helpful to youngsters who do not yet have racing stop watches. Just shout it out through your megaphone, or over the public address system if you have one.

Keep track of the winners and the order of finish, and post them on your class bulletin board. This recognition is extremely important and should be done for all events whenever possible. Two or three informal races at the end of each day's lesson in boats will be a highlight of your program, as far as the students are concerned.

Short races teach best. Whether triangular or windward-leeward, the short course is best. Marks can even be as close as fifteen or twenty boat lengths. There is less work for the instructor in setting out the course and less work to patrol it while students race.

More important, however, the short course is best in that it gives the student more contact with other boats. He has to maneuver often and must put each rule into effect many times. Since the racing time is cut down, more races can be held each day and the amount of competitive work increased considerably.

If you wish, you can make the races two or three laps around, then patrol the course and continue coaching individual skippers on general seamanship. A station near the weather mark is particularly good for observing tacking procedures, ability to trim sails for beating and reaching, and racing rules.

Encourage protesting when your class gets into racing rules and tactics. The protest committee can be an elected group from the class itself, who can read the rules and make the judgments. Avoid

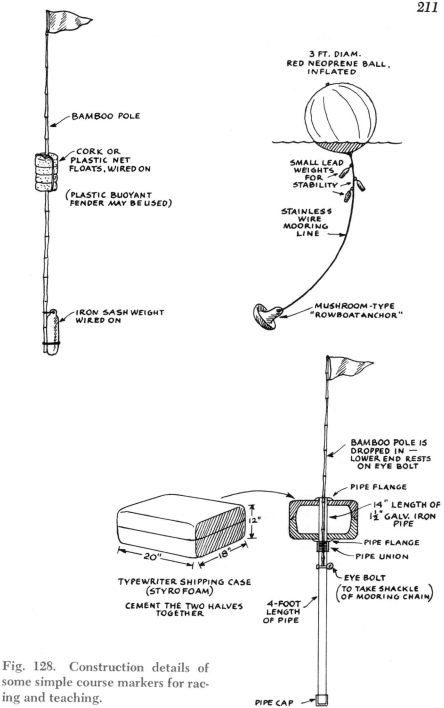

Fig. 128. Construction details of some simple course markers for racing and teaching.

making any snap judgments yourself; let the youngsters figure it out, and they'll learn it.

How to make course markers. For teaching purposes the course markers can be small, which greatly reduces the work for you or whoever has to put them out and take them in. Some simple types made of inexpensive odds and ends are shown in Fig. 128.

The balloon marker is the easiest to handle and is suitable for work with beginners. The long fish-pole markers can be of any height and are good for larger racing courses since they can be easily seen a half mile or more away.

5. Programs for a rainy day. Rain may be the farmer's friend, but it is the enemy of the sailing instructor. Keeping twenty or thirty energetic boys and girls inside on a rainy day is a monumental task. It can be done if you break your lectures and quizzes up with things to do in which the students can participate actively.

Working with knots, splices, and whippings will help the students get off their benches and stir their legs. A demonstration and contest in heaving lines can be done inside. If the rain is more of a slow drizzle than a downpour, this may be the time to get in some instruction and practice in rowing. A little dampness won't hurt anyone, but better let the students sit on dry cushions or life jackets.

With advanced planning a field trip to a marina or boat yard has merit, or to a sail loft if there is one nearby. These should be scheduled first with the proprietors, of course. Occasionally a good sailing movie can be found, or a private film from someone who has just completed an interesting cruise.

Instruction in securing boats at the dock can be done in rainy weather, with emphasis on precautions to take for lines' shrinking and on how to prepare for bad storms. Good and bad examples of boat mooring can probably be found on most water fronts.

When out in wet weather, warn your students about the slippery docks; they can be treacherous, so walk, don't run.

6. Promoting the racing fleets. From the sailing class, the students should progress into the racing fleets, but some groundwork must be laid in advance: interest.

Whenever possible, advanced students should be given opportunity to crew with racing skippers, and instructors should work hard to find them berths. As often as possible the racing skipper should let the student take the tiller and try his hand in a larger boat. This should be done on a day with good winds and plenty of excitement . . . and the fleet will gain a new convert.

Crew races. For your own racing groups, make sure that crews get some time to act as skippers. At San Diego there is a crew's race every day — a fine morale builder. In the beginner and interme-diate classes skippers and crews should be alternating jobs through-out the course of the day, so both receive the same instruction.

SUMMARY OF METHODS USED
IN TEACHING SAILING SUCCESSFULLY:

  (1) Keep lectures short and to the point
  (2) Make lectures explain, show, and summarize
  (3) Use teaching aids and demonstrations
  (4) Stress safety at all times
  (5) Maintain strict discipline when on the water
  (6) Keep boats together by using single-file method
  (7) Brief instructors on each day's lesson beforehand
  (8) Begin racing early and keep scores
  (9) Use small courses and many races
 (10) Praise frequently, go over mistakes publicly, but criticize seldom
 (11) Use oral and written examinations
 (12) Award trophies and diplomas wherever possible

APPENDIX A
Answers to Questions

Chapter 1, page 29

1. (a) Upper railing of the boat. (b) Line controlling the sail. (c) A pulley. (d) Wood or metal piece in center of boat, which acts as keel. (e) A rope eye spliced over a metal thimble, in part of sail.

2. Rigging that supports mast and does not move.

3. Mast and boom.

4. Sheets and halyards, and other lines which move.

5. (1) Mast (2) Luff of sail (3) Forestay (4) Centerboard trunk (5) Centerboard (6) Transom (7) Traveler (8) Sheet (9) Outhaul (10) Batten

6. The steering mechanism. Tiller or wheel.

7. Bolt· rope is sewn to sail. Attaches along foot and luff.

8. (1) Lower centerboard (2) Fasten rudder and tiller (3) Put on sail (4) Shackle halyard (5) Put in battens (6) Clear mainsheet (7) Tie figure-8 knot (8) Look aloft, hoist sail

9. (1) Astern (2) Stern (3) Starboard side (4) Ahead (5) Aft, or abaft

10. (a) True   (f) False
    (b) False   (g) True
    (c) False   (h) False
    (d) True   (i) False
    (e) True   (j) False

Chapter 2, page 47

1. (a) Running   (d) Beating
    (b) Beating   (e) Running
    (c) Reaching   (f) Running
                  (g) Reaching

2. Lateral resistance. Provided by centerboard, also by rudder and hull.

3. You make leeway, because of loss of lateral resistance.

4. (a) The luff of the sail. (b) Sternway. (c) Down. (d) Moves the bow to starboard. (e) Some point near the middle.

5. If closer, the normal curve of the sail begins to luff.

6. Direction of the wind; heading of the boat; trim of the sails.

7. Trim to close-hauled. Ease up until sail just luffs. Wind is at 45 degrees to boat's heading.

8. Trees blowing; chimney smoke; cat's paws on water; flags on houses or masts; boats at anchor; boats sailing; pennants and telltales; cool side of wet finger, or face.

9. (a) False   (f) True
    (b) False   (g) True
    (c) True   (h) True
    (d) False   (i) False
    (e) True   (j) False

10. (a) Sailing as close to the wind as possible. (b) Loosen or slack off on the sheet. (c) Side away from wind. (d) Side toward the wind. (e) Tacking downwind. (f) Tacking upwind. (g) Side away from the wind. (h) Changing course more into the wind. (i) Boom is over starboard side. (j) Boom is over port side.

Chapter 3, page 59

1. (a) Any heading where bow is more into wind than away from it. (b) Change in the wind direction. (c) Ability to sail close-hauled. (d) Hard over to the lee side. (e) Luffing head-to-wind, with no way on.

2. Use the luff of the sail to tell you when and how the wind shifts.

3. Find wind direction, and sail about 45 degrees to it; trim sail close-hauled; head up slowly into wind; fall off slightly at first luff.

4. Further ahead, called a "header." Test wind by easing up into it.

5. (a) Pinching. (b) Easing sheet. (c) Heading up slowly. (d) Near the mast.

6. (1) c; (2) b; (3) a; (4) d; (5) f.

7. Push tiller and boom to one side or the other, gather sternway, and then steer off on one tack.

8. (a) False   (f) False
    (b) True   (g) True
    (c) False   (h) False
    (d) False   (i) False
    (e) True   (j) True

Chapter 4, page 71

1. It is easier to sail upwind while the wind is strong, and you can always drift home on a run if the wind drops.

2. On a run, the wind comes from the same side the sail is on. It may lead to accidental jibe.

3. (a) Down. (b) On a broad reach, or directly downwind. (c) Sheet.
4. (1) d; (2) a; (3) b; (4) e; (5) f; (6) g.
5. (a) B; (b) A; (c) D; (d) A, C.
6. (a) Trim it in. (b) Let it out. (c) Change heading and fall off.
7. Controlling sail at all times, keeping wind dead astern or on windward quarter (broad reaching).
8. Turn boat around so bow is heading into wind, have someone shove you off by pushing on boom. With boats on each side, get shoved off with hard push to gather sternway, and steer out.
9. Tie with a stern anchor; use fenders or cushions on both sides; use leeward side of dock; moor out; use stern line to other boat, shore, or piling.
10. (a) True   (f) False
    (b) False   (g) False
    (c) False   (h) False
    (d) True   (i) True
    (e) True

Chapter 5, page 81
1. Crew should be swimmer, for safety and because non-swimmer has instinctive fear of water.
2. Hike out to windward; head up into wind; luff sail.
3. In case of trouble, it cannot be released quickly or when wet.
4. Life jackets are kept someplace where they can be gotten out easily, such as under the seat. Halyard is coiled and stowed near foot of mast, on starboard side. Sheet is kept on floor of cockpit.
5. Find crew first. You cannot duck under water with life jacket on. Stay with the boat always.
6. Untie halyards and sheets. Remove sails. Right boat. Stuff rope or rags in centerboard well and bail out. If necessary, unstep mast.
7. (a) Start at once, even if in bottom of boat. (b) Pull jaw up and back. (c) Fend off with his feet. (d) Bulky but warm.
8. (a) False   (d) False
   (b) True   (e) False
   (c) True   (f) False
                  (g) True

Chapter 6, page 97
1. (a) Flags or other objects marking race course. (b) Boats designed and built to the same specifications. (c) Three legs to the course. (d) Two legs, in line with

wind. (e) Imaginary line between first marker and race committee boat. (f) Port and starboard tack. (g) Both boats on port or both on starboard.
2. (a) Taking the mark to starboard. (b) Port side. (c) Any part. (d) When the red flag or signal is hoisted. (e) Four and a half. (f) The race committee will tell you.
3. It is accurate, and it can be set for the minutes to go with the starting flags.
4. See Chapter 6, or Appendix B for full definitions.
5. (a) False   (e) True
   (b) False   (f) True
   (c) True   (g) False
   (d) False
6. These boats must give way or keep clear:
A, opposite tack rule; C, tacking and jibing rule; E, passing marks rule; G, same tack rule, overtaking boat; H, same tack rule, windward boat; K, opposite tack rule; M, same tack rule, windward boat; P, opposite tack rule.

Chapter 7, page 114
1. (a) Whitecaps. (b) Triangular, red. (c) Waterproof jacket, waterproof pants or bathing suit, heavy sweater. (d) Tighter. (e) Hiking out, heading up, luffing sail.
2. (a) Weather helm. Shift weight aft. (b) Dark and dirty bottom. (c) Half an hour. (d) Wind.
3. b, c, d.
4. a, c.
5. (a) Small cords sewn into grommets, for reefing sail. (b) Large rings at end of reef points. (c) A method of rolling sail on boom to reef. (d) Smaller and heavier sails for bad weather. (e) Canvas funnel towed in water during storm.
6. Head up into puffs, so you are working up to windward. Note direction of wind in puffs, so you can predict a wind shift.
7. Usually the waves are not so rough and the water is smoother. If you should capsize, you are also closer to help.
8. No; sailing directly downwind in heavy puffs is dangerous, because it is easy to jibe accidentally.
9. Round up to a beat, come about, then fall off to a broad reach or run.
10. (a) True   (f) True
    (b) True   (g) False
    (c) True   (h) True
    (d) True   (i) True
    (e) False   (j) False

Chapter 8, page 122

1. (a) L (f) L
   (b) L (g) S
   (c) S (h) S
   (d) L (i) S, L
   (e) L, S
2. Bow line, mainsheet, seaweed on rudder or centerboard, fenders, hands or feet.
3. Smooth with fine grade wet sandpaper, finish with soap and water or fine abrasive like rottenstone.
4. Sail will set better for the light wind, and boat will be able to foot instead of pointing.
5. Anchor when current starts moving you back (sternway). It is permitted.
6. Smoke on shore, cloud formations or thunderheads, boats moving in distance, streaks of dark water, movement of cigarette smoke in boat, cliffs or gorges of the shoreline, afternoon offshore breezes.
7. (a) False (f) True
   (b) False (g) True
   (c) True   (h) True
   (d) True   (i) False
   (e) False

Chapter 9, page 134

1. Trying to claim buoy room on a boat close-hauled at the starting mark. Usually done by a boat approaching start on reach.
2. See text in Chapter 9. No, applies at start only. Yes, it applies after start signal is given.
3. See text in Chapter 9. Yes, applies to all boats on wrong side of line at start signal.
4. These boats will have to give way or keep clear: A, B, anti-barging rule; E, F, over line early rule; I, opposite tack rule; L, same tack rule, windward boat; M, over line early rule; O, P, anti-barging rule.
5. (a) Have full headway. (b) There are boats to leeward of you. (c) Luff sail now to slow down. (d) Sail your own race and let him give you room (e) Make your run shorter.
6. Range marker helps you keep on close-hauled course at same place on line. Use it when running away from line, to stay on this course.
7. The end closer into the wind. Luff dead into wind at middle of line.
8. (a) False (f) True
   (b) True   (g) True
   (c) True   (h) True
   (d) True   (i) False
   (e) False

Chapter 10, page 154

1. An eye or fitting through which a line runs to change its direction.
2. To keep the boat headed into wind by leaving mainsail up longer.
3. Jib is trimmed too tight.
4. Ease jib sheet. Trim main sheet.
5. When the jib has a sizable luff, or "breaks."
6. Gives mast fore and aft support, allows a lighter mast.
7. Skimming over top of water (on one's own bow wave) at nearly double speed, while sailing to leeward.
8. Sail it flat. Fall off. Trim mainsail in rapidly.
9. (1) Headstay; (2) Jibstay; (3) Backstay; (4) Spreader; (5) Lower shroud; (6) Backstay track; (7) Jib fair lead; (8) Tack; (9) Clew; (10) Jib snap; (11) Jib halyard; (12) Miter; (13) Chine; (14) Telltale; (15) Turnbuckle.
10. Mainsail hoisted first. Jib next. Jib down first. This keeps mainsail up longest, for weather-vane effect.
11. (a) False (l) True
    (b) False (m) False
    (c) True   (n) True
    (d) True   (o) False
    (e) False (p) False
    (f) False (q) True
    (g) True   (r) True
    (h) True   (s) False
    (i) False (t) False
    (j) False (u) True
    (k) False (v) True

Chapter 11, page 171

1. (a) Erosive action of sea water on two dissimilar metals. (b) A plastic (spun glass) of great strength and durability, used on many boat hulls. (c) Adjusting and caring for boat. (d) The wheel of a pulley. (e) Wedges supporting dinghy when on dock or ship. (f) Lower part of boat's hull, where water inside will collect. (g) Drain hole between ribs. (h) Up, or high above deck. (i) Amount mast is tipped fore and aft. (j) A fitting through which sheet runs to change its direction. (k) Boat tends to round up to windward, if tiller let go. (l) Shrouds which begin and end on mast, in pattern of a diamond. (m) Wind deflected from the windward side of jib, or from another boat's sail. (n) Making sail fast to boom, mast, other rigging. (o) Tall masts with triangular sails, also called jib-headed and Bermudian rigs.

2. (a) Dry salt will collect moisture, causing mildew and corrosion. (b) Yes. Pull up on jib sheet to change angle of lead. (c) To leeward. (d) Let mainsail out, move weight aft, swing centerboard aft, reduce any rake aft in mast. (e) By reading, practicing, and racing all you can.
3. a, b, d, f, g, h, k, l, m.
4. Total: 9. Time gained: 90 seconds, or 1½ minutes. Boats beaten: 10.
5. (a) False   (i) True
   (b) True   (j) False
   (c) True   (k) False
   (d) True   (l) True
   (e) False   (m) True
   (f) True   (n) True
   (g) False   (o) False
   (h) True

Chapter 12, page 183

1. (a) Near the side of the boat. (b) Be able to make a windward mark without having to tack. (c) Sailing farther than is needed to fetch the mark. (d) Tacking excessively on the windward leg, without reason. (e) Moving tiller rapidly from side to side. (f) Deflected wind from windward side of jib or other boat's sail. (g) Putting another boat in the lee of your sail. (h) The direction wind *seems to be blowing* when boat is underway. Same as direction of wind pennant. (i) A position to leeward and forward of another boat's blanket zone. (j) A crisscrossing of waves, turbulent water, often caused by many boats being in small area.
2. Follow illustrations in text, Chapter 12.
3. (a) Moving tiller side to side in a regular manner. Harmful. It slows boat. (b) Boats ahead. They will show effect of new winds; also, they are usually the better skippers. (c) To sail hard every minute of the race. (d) This slows the boat by acting as a drag. (e) It can luff the other boat into the wind, prevent passing. More effective on reach.
4. (a) False   (k) False
   (b) True   (l) False
   (c) False   (m) False
   (d) False   (n) True
   (e) True   (o) False
   (f) True   (p) True
   (g) True   (q) False
   (h) True   (r) True
   (i) False   (s) False
   (j) True   (t) True

Chapter 13, page 192

1. (a) More wake, backwind, choppy water, and disturbed air. (b) Avoid the crowds, unless you are an expert skipper. (c) Which end of starting line seems better, where windward mark is, and how the wind varies on the windward leg, etc. (d) Safely, yes, but you should not sail here as this interferes with the other classes' starts. You cannot sail to leeward of the line when they are starting; this is the restricted area.
2. (a) False   (i) True
   (b) False   (j) True
   (c) False   (k) True
   (d) False   (l) True
   (e) True   (m) False
   (f) True   (n) True
   (g) True   (o) False
   (h) True

APPENDIX B
Official Racing Rules

The following are portions of the racing rules of the North American Yacht Racing Union, adopted 1965, and are reprinted with permission. Complete copies of the official Racing Rules may be obtained from Corresponding Secretary, 37 West 44th Street, New York, New York 10036.

Listed below are excerpts from those sections of the rules of most interest to junior sailors and racing skippers.

PART 1: DEFINITIONS

Racing—A yacht is **racing** from her preparatory signal until she has either **finished** and cleared the finishing line and finishing **marks** or retired, or until the race has been **cancelled, postponed,** or **abandoned,** except that in match or team races, the sailing instructions may prescribe that a yacht is **racing** from any specified time before the preparatory signal.

Starting—A yacht starts when, after her starting signal, any part of her hull, crew or equipment first crosses the starting line in the direction of the first mark.

Finishing—A yacht finishes when any part of her hull, or of her crew or equipment in normal position, crosses the finishing line from the direction of the last mark.

Luffing—Altering course towards the wind until head to wind.

Tacking—A yacht is **tacking** from the moment she is beyond head to wind until she has **borne away**, if beating to windward, to a **close-hauled** course; if not beating to windward, to the course on which her mainsail has filled.

Bearing Away—Altering course away from the wind until a yacht begins to jibe.

Jibing—A yacht begins to **jibe** at the moment when, with the wind aft, the foot of her mainsail crosses her center line and completes the **jibe** when the mainsail has filled on the other **tack**.

On a Tack—A yacht is **on a tack** except when she is **tacking** or **jibing**. A yacht is **on the tack (starboard** or **port)** corresponding to her windward side.

Close-hauled—A yacht is **close-hauled** when sailing by the wind as close as she can lie with advantage in working to windward.

Leeward and **Windward**—The **leeward** side of a yacht is that on which she is, or, if **luffing** head to wind, was, carrying her mainsail. The opposite side is the **windward** side.

When neither of two yachts on the same **tack is clear astern**, the one on the **leeward** side of the other is the **leeward yacht**. The other is the **windward yacht**.

Clear Astern and **Clear Ahead; Overlap**—A yacht is **clear astern** of another when her hull and equipment are abaft an imaginary line projected abeam from the aftermost point of the other's hull and equipment. The other yacht is **clear ahead**. The yachts **overlap** if neither is **clear astern**; or if, although one is **clear astern**, an intervening yacht **overlaps** both of them. The terms **clear astern**, **clear ahead** and **overlap** apply to yachts on opposite **tacks** only when they are subject to rule 42—Rounding or Passing Marks and Obstructions.

Proper Course—A **proper course** is any course which a yacht might sail after the starting signal, in the absence of the other yacht or yachts affected, to **finish** as quickly as possible. The course sailed before **luffing** or **bearing away** is presumably,

but not necessarily, that yacht's **proper course**. There is no **proper course** before the starting signal.

Mark—A mark is any object specified in the sailing instructions which a yacht must round or pass on a required side.

Obstruction—An **obstruction** is any object, including craft under way, large enough to require a yacht, if not less than one overall length away from it, to make a substantial alteration of course to pass on one side or the other, or any object which can be passed on one side only, including a buoy when the yacht in question cannot safely pass between it and the shoal or object which it marks.

PART IV: SAILING RULES WHEN YACHTS MEET
SECTION A—RULES WHICH ALWAYS APPLY

31—Disqualification

1. A yacht may be disqualified for infringing a rule of Part IV only when the infringement occurs while she is **racing**, whether or not a collision results.

2. A yacht may be disqualified before or after she is **racing** for seriously hindering a yacht which is **racing**, or for infringing the sailing instructions.

32—Avoiding Collisions

A right-of-way yacht which makes no attempt to avoid a collision resulting in serious damage may be disqualified as well as the other yacht.

33—Retiring from Race

A yacht, which realizes she has infringed a racing rule or a sailing instruction, should retire promptly; but, if she persists in racing, other yachts shall continue to accord her such rights as she may have under the rules of Part IV.

34—Misleading or Balking

1. When one yacht is required to keep clear of another, the right-of-way yacht shall not (except to the extent permitted by rule 38.1, Luffing after Starting), so alter course as to:—
(a) prevent the other yacht from keeping clear; or
(b) mislead or balk her while she is keeping clear.

2. A yacht is not misleading or balking another if she alters course by **luffing** or **bearing away** to conform to a change in the strength or direction of the wind.

35—Hailing

A right-of-way yacht, except when luffing under rule 38.1, Luffing after Starting, should hail before or when making an alteration of course which may not be foreseen by the other yacht or when claiming room at a **mark** or **obstruction**.

SECTION B—OPPOSITE TACK RULE
36—Fundamental Rule
A **port-tack** yacht shall keep clear of a **starboard-tack** yacht.

SECTION C—SAME TACK RULES
37—Fundamental Rules
1. A **windward yacht** shall keep clear of a **leeward yacht**.
2. A yacht **clear astern** shall keep clear of a yacht **clear ahead**.
3. A yacht which establishes an **overlap** to **leeward** from **clear astern** shall allow the **windward yacht** ample room and opportunity to keep clear, and during the existence of that **overlap** the **leeward** yacht shall not sail above her **proper course**.
38—Right-of-Way Yacht Luffing after Starting
1. **Luffing Rights and Limitations.** After she has **started** and cleared the starting line, a yacht **clear ahead** or a **leeward yacht** may **luff** as she pleases, except that:—

A **leeward yacht** shall not sail above her **proper course** while an **overlap** exists if, at any time during its existence, the helmsman of the **windward yacht** (when sighting abeam from his normal station and sailing no higher than the **leeward yacht**) has been abreast or forward of the mainmast of the **leeward yacht**.
2. **Overlap Limitations.** For the purpose of this rule: an **overlap** does not exist unless the yachts are clearly within two overall lengths of the longer yacht; and an **overlap** which exists between two yachts when the leading yacht **starts**, or when one or both of them completes a **tack** or **jibe**, shall be regarded as a new **overlap** beginning at that time.
3. **Hailing to Stop or Prevent a Luff.** When there is doubt, the **leeward yacht** may assume that she has the right to **luff** unless the helmsman of the **windward yacht** has hailed "Mast Abeam," or words to that effect. The **leeward yacht** shall be governed by such hail, and, if she deems it improper, her only remedy is to protest.
4. **Curtailing a Luff.** The **windward yacht** shall not cause a **luff** to be curtailed because of her proximity to the **leeward yacht** unless an **obstruction**, a third yacht or other object restricts her ability to respond.
5. **Luffing Two or More Yachts.** A yacht

shall not **luff** unless she has the right to **luff** all yachts which would be affected by her **luff**, in which case they shall all respond even if an intervening yacht or yachts would not otherwise have the right to **luff**.
39—Sailing Below a Proper Course after Starting
A yacht which is on a free leg of the course after having **started** and cleared the starting line shall not sail below her **proper course** when she is clearly within three of her overall lengths of either a **leeward yacht** or a yacht **clear astern** which is steering a course to pass to **leeward**.
40—Right-of-Way Yacht Luffing before Starting
Before a yacht has **started** and cleared the starting line, any **luff** on her part which affects another yacht shall be carried out slowly. A **leeward yacht** may so **luff** only when the helmsman of the **windward yacht** (sighting abeam from his normal station) is abaft the mainmast of the **leeward yacht**. However, after her starting signal the **leeward yacht** may **luff** slowly to assume her **proper course** even when, because of her position, she would not otherwise have the right to **luff**. Rules 38.3, Hailing to Stop or Prevent a Luff; 38.4, Curtailing a Luff; and 38.5, Luffing Two or More Yachts, also apply.

SECTION D—CHANGING TACK RULES
41—Tacking or Jibing
1. A yacht which is either **tacking** or **jibing** shall keep clear of a yacht **on a tack**.
2. A yacht shall neither **tack** nor **jibe** into a position which will give her right of way unless she does so far enough from a yacht **on a tack** to enable this yacht to keep clear without having to begin to alter her course until after the **tack** or **jibe** has been completed.
3. A yacht which **tacks** or **jibes** has the onus of satisfying the Race Committee that she completed her **tack** or **jibe** in accordance with rule 41.2.
4. When two yachts are both **tacking** or both **jibing** at the same time, the one on the other's **port** side shall keep clear.

SECTION E—RULES OF EXCEPTION AND SPECIAL APPLICATION
When a rule of this section applies, to the extent to which it explicitly provides rights and obligations, it overrides any conflicting rule of Part IV which precedes it, except the rules of Section A—Rules Which Always Apply.

42—Rounding or Passing Marks and Obstructions

When yachts either on the same tack or, after starting and clearing the starting line, on opposite tacks, are about to round or pass a mark on the same required side or an obstruction on the same side:—

When Overlapped

1. (a) An outside yacht shall give each yacht overlapping her on the inside room to round or pass it, except as provided in rules 42.1(c), (d) and (e). Room includes room to tack or jibe when either is an integral part of the rounding or passing maneuver.

(b) When an inside yacht of two or more overlapped yachts on opposite tacks will have to jibe in rounding a mark, in order most directly to assume a proper course on the next leg, she shall jibe when she has obtained room.

(c) When two yachts on opposite tacks are either on a beat or when one of them will have to tack either to round the mark or to avoid the obstruction, as between each other rule 42.1(a) shall not apply and they are subject to rules 36, Opposite Tack Fundamental Rule, and 41, Tacking or Jibing.

(d) An outside leeward yacht with luffing rights may take an inside yacht to windward of a mark provided that she hails to that effect and begins to luff before she is within two of her overall lengths of the mark and provided that she also passes to windward of it.

(e) (Anti-Barging Rule) When approaching the starting line to start, a leeward yacht shall be under no obligation to give any windward yacht room to pass to leeward of a starting mark surrounded by navigable water; but, after the starting signal, a leeward yacht shall not deprive a windward yacht of room at such mark either:—

(i) by heading above the first mark; or

(ii) by luffing above close-hauled.

When Clear Astern and Clear Ahead

2. (a) A yacht clear astern shall keep clear in anticipation of and during the rounding or passing maneuver when the yacht clear ahead remains on the same tack or jibes.

(b) A yacht clear ahead which tacks to round a mark is subject to rule 41, Tacking or Jibing, but a yacht clear astern shall not luff above close-hauled so as to prevent the yacht clear ahead from tacking.

Restrictions on Establishing and Breaking an Overlap

3. (a) A yacht clear astern shall not establish an inside overlap and be entitled to room under rule 42.1(a) when the yacht clear ahead:

(i) is within two of her own lengths of the mark or obstruction, except as provided in rule 42.3(b); or

(ii) is unable to give the required room.

(b) A yacht clear astern may establish an overlap between the yacht clear ahead and a continuing obstruction such as a shoal or the shore, only when there is room for her to do so in safety.

(c) A yacht clear ahead shall be under no obligation to give room before an overlap is established. The onus will lie upon the yacht which has been clear astern to satisfy the Race Committee that the overlap was established in proper time.

(d) When an overlap exists at the time the outside yacht comes within two of her lengths of the mark, she shall nevertheless be bound by rule 42.1(a), even though the overlap may thereafter be broken.

43—Close-hauled, Hailing for Room to Tack at Obstructions

1. Hailing. When safe pilotage requires one of two close-hauled yachts on the same tack to make a substantial alteration of course to clear an obstruction, and if she intends to tack, but cannot tack without colliding with the other yacht, she shall hail the other yacht for room to tack.

2. Responding. The hailed yacht at the earliest possible moment after the hail shall either:—

(a) tack, in which case, the hailing yacht shall begin to tack either:—

(i) before the hailed yacht has completed her tack, or

(ii) if she cannot then tack without colliding with the hailed yacht, immediately she is able to tack, or

(b) reply "You tack," or words to that effect, if in her opinion she can keep clear without tacking or after postponing her tack. In this case:—

(i) the hailing yacht shall immediately tack and

(ii) the hailed yacht shall keep clear.

(iii) The onus shall lie on the hailed yacht which replied "You **tack**" to satisfy the Race Committee that she kept clear.

3. **Limitation on Right to Room**
(a) When the **obstruction** is a **mark** which the hailed yacht can fetch, the hailing yacht shall not be entitled to room to **tack** and the hailed yacht shall immediately so inform the hailing yacht.

(b) If, thereafter, the hailing yacht again hails for room to **tack**, she shall, after receiving it, retire immediately.

(c) If, after having refused to respond to a hail under rule 43.3(a), the hailed yacht fails to fetch, she shall retire immediately.

44—Yachts Returning to Start
1. (a) A premature starter when returning to **start**, or a yacht working into position from the wrong side of the starting line or its extensions, when the starting signal is made, shall keep clear of all yachts which are **starting**, or have **started**, correctly, until she is wholly on the right side of the starting line or its extensions.

(b) Thereafter, she shall be accorded the rights under the rules of Part IV of a yacht which is **starting** correctly; but if she thereby acquires right of way over another yacht which is **starting** correctly, she shall allow that yacht ample room and opportunity to keep clear.

2. A premature starter while continuing to sail the course and until it is obvious that she is returning to **start**, shall be accorded the rights under the rules of Part IV of a yacht which has **started**.

45—Anchored, Aground or Capsized
1. A yacht under way shall keep clear of another yacht **racing** which is anchored, aground or capsized. Of two anchored yachts, the one which anchored later shall keep clear, except that a yacht which is dragging shall keep clear of one which is not.

2. A yacht anchored or aground shall indicate the fact to any yacht which may be in danger of fouling her. Unless the size of the yachts or the weather conditions make some other signal necessary, a hail is sufficient indication.

3. A yacht shall not be penalized for fouling a yacht in distress which she is attempting to assist nor a yacht which goes aground or capsized immediately ahead of her.

PART V: OTHER SAILING RULES
49—Fair Sailing
A yacht shall attempt to win a race only by fair sailing, superior speed and skill, and, except in team races, by individual effort. However, a yacht may be disqualified under this rule only in the case of a clear-cut violation of the above principles and only if no other rule applies.

50—Ranking as a Starter
A yacht which sails about in the vicinity of the starting line between her preparatory and starting signals shall rank as a starter, even if she does not **start**.

51—Sailing the Course
1. (a) A yacht shall **start** and **finish** only as prescribed in the starting and finishing definitions, even if the committee boat is anchored on the side of the starting or finishing **mark** opposite to that prescribed in the sailing instructions.

(b) Unless otherwise prescribed in the sailing instructions, a yacht which either crosses prematurely, or is on the wrong side of the starting line at the starting signal, or at any other prescribed time before the starting signal, shall return and **start** in accordance with the definition.

(c) Failure of a yacht to see or hear her recall notification shall not relieve her of her obligation of **starting** correctly.

2. A yacht shall sail the course so as to round or pass each **mark** on the required side in correct sequence, so that a string representing her wake from the time she **starts** until she **finishes** would, when drawn taut, lie on the required side of each **mark**.

3. A **mark** has a required side for a yacht as long as she is on a leg which it begins, bounds or ends. A starting **mark** begins to have a required side for a yacht when she **starts**. A finishing **mark** ceases to have a required side for a yacht as soon as she **finishes**.

4. A yacht which rounds or passes a **mark** on the wrong side may correct her error by making her course conform to the requirements of rule 51.2.

5. It is not necessary for a yacht to cross the finishing line completely. After **finishing** she may clear it in either direction.

6. In the absence of the Race Commit-

tee, a yacht shall take her own time when she finishes, and report the time taken to the Race Committee as soon as possible. If there is no longer an established finishing line, the finishing line shall be a line extending from the required side of the finishing mark, at right angles to the last leg of the course, and 100 yards long or as much longer as may be necessary to insure adequate depth of water in crossing it.

52—Touching a Mark

1. A yacht which either:—
    (a) touches:—
        (i) a starting **mark** before **starting**;
        (ii) a **mark** which begins, bounds

or ends the leg of the course on which she is sailing; or
    (iii) a finishing **mark** after **finishing**, or
    (b) causes a **mark** vessel to shift to avoid being touched, shall retire immediately, unless she claims that she was wrongfully compelled to touch it by another yacht, in which case she shall protest.

2. For the purposes of rule 52.1: Every ordinary part of a **mark** ranks as part of it, including a flag, flagpole, boom or hoisted boat, but excluding ground tackle and any object either accidentally or temporarily attached to it.

INDEX